Feasting in the Wilderness

The Lord's Supper in Early North American Methodism

D. Gregory Van Dussen

EMETH PRESS
www.emethpress.com

FEASTING IN THE WILDERNESS: The Lord's Supper in Early North American Methodism

Copyright © 2025 D. Gregory Van Dussen
Printed in the United States of America on acid-free paper

All rights reserved. No part of this book may be reproduced, or stored in a retrieval system or transmitted in any form or by any means, electronic, mechanical, photocopying, recording, scanning or otherwise, except as permitted by the 1976 United States Copyright Act, or with the prior written permission of Emeth Press. Requests for permission should be addressed to: Emeth Press, P. O. Box 533, Jackson, Georgia 30233.   http://www.emethpress.com.

Library of Congress Control Number 2025036769

ISBN 9781609472160

COVER ART

Many thanks to Mary Khalil of Co. Clare, Ireland, for her artwork on the cover. The wild grapes represent an improvised camp meeting Communion, held in the wilderness of the Ozark Mountains, described by Rev. Henry C. Benson [1815-97].

Endorsements

Gregory Van Dussen continues his important work of allowing the circuit riders to speak to us today. While many of us would associate such servants of God with evangelistic preaching and revivalistic services, Van Dussen highlights the central place of the Lord's Supper in circuit rider spirituality. Beginning with early Methodism in Britain, he traces the lineage of this communion-centered spirituality across the Atlantic to the far-flung mission of the circuit riders in North America. As he shows, this great cloud of witnesses still has much to teach us!

  - **James E. Pedlar, Bastian Chair of Wesley Studies, Tyndale Seminary**

Drawing upon his deep familiarity with the personalities and primary documents of early North American Methodism, historian Greg Van Dussen has produced a valuable survey of Eucharistic practices among Methodists living in frontier settings in the racially polarized southern United States, through the trans-Appalachian region, to sparsely populated and yet racially diverse Upper Canada. Van Dussen gives us vivid examples of the efforts of early Methodist leaders to satisfy the hunger for sacramental care among people living in frontier settlements, as well as powerful contemporary accounts of the results when these needs were met. While giving due attention to the failings of Christian people, *Feasting in the Wilderness* focuses on the larger story of the unfailing – and often surprising - grace of God made visible in the lives of ordinary people of all races who lived in the American borderlands and the committed and faithful ministers of all races who cared for them wherever they were to be found.

  - **Elizabeth K. Lynch, Assistant to the Editor, Bibliographical Society of the University of Virginia**

D. Gregory Van Dussen's *Feasting in the Wilderness* is a master class in the history, theology, and practice of the Sacrament of Holy Communion in North American Methodism. Deeply grounded in the careful nuances of John and Charles Wesley's sacramental theology, Van Dussen deftly narrates the story of the centrality of the Lord's Supper in eighteenth and nineteenth-century American and Canadian Methodism. Van Dussen's vigilant recounting provides a much needed corrective to the common misconception that a high view of the sacraments cannot coexist with a passionate commitment to the evangelistic calling of the church. Indeed, Van Dussen illustrates with crystal clarity that the most distinctive charism of historic Methodism was its unwavering insistence on holding together, in creative tension, a commitment to both a sacramental and an evangelical theology. In the early years of Methodism, these were not seen as separate paths, but an integrated tour de force of the Gospel's transforming grace. Feasting in the Wilderness provides a fitting crescendo to Van Dussen's previous volumes on camp meetings and circuit riders in the Methodist movement. He shows the climactic significance and centrality of Eucharist services in the spreading of the Gospel across the North American frontier. D. Gregory Van Dussen is a master teacher. One cannot read Feasting in the Wilderness without wondering whether Methodism can survive in the twenty-first century and beyond without a full-orbed recovery of the inseparable relationship between the Holy Eucharist and the transformational Gospel of Christ. Highly recommended.

- Douglas R. Cullum, Ph.D., Vice President and Dean Emeritus; Professor of Historical and Pastoral Theology, Northeastern Seminary, Rochester, NY

This book is a helpful survey of the attitudes and practices of early Methodists in regards to the eucharist or Lord's Supper. The book has two parts. The first establishes the importance of the sacrament for the Wesleys and for Adam Clarke, one of Methodism's first interpreters. The second part examines the practice of the sacrament among Methodists in the United States and Canada. Relying heavily on anecdotes, the author demonstrates that participation in communion, especially in connection with camp meetings, was a vital part of the Methodist experience.

- John Oswalt, Asbury Theological Seminary

Dedication

I am more than happy to dedicate this book to my wife Jackie, whose encouragement and practical assistance have made this book possible.

Table of Contents

Acknowledgements / xi

Dedication / xiii

Foreword / xv

Introduction / 1

Chapter 1
  John Wesley and Adam Clarke on the importance of Eucharistic Worship / 9

Chapter 2
  Eucharistic Hymns of John and Charles Wesley / 27

Chapter 3
  John Wesley's Hope and Provision for American Methodist Worship / 43

Chapter 4
  The Lord's Supper in Early North American Methodism / 47

Chapter 5
  "Until He Comes" (I Corinthians 11:26) / 75

APPENDIX
  Fencing the Lord's Table / 91

Foreword

It is an honor to write this foreword, having been asked to do so by long term friend and colleague D. Gregory Van Dussen. Both Greg and I have devoted our professional lives as pastors to the revitalization of Methodism through theological renewal. My path has been as pastor of several United Methodist churches where I and the lay leadership laid a foundation of Wesleyan theology and thereby proved that such theological renewal clearly produced fruit for God's Kingdom. God honored that decision in each parish setting. Then for eight years I served as District Superintendent of the Cornerstone District in the Western New York and Upper New York Annual Conferences, encouraging the pastors in the district to follow through with establishing or continuing a similar theological foundation in their appointments. During that period I was also involved with the renewal movement The Confessing Movement with The United Methodist Church and served a term as the President of the Board of Directors. The Confessing Movement aimed to reaffirm traditional Wesleyan theology within The United Methodist Church. It is from this experience that I wholeheartedly endorse the book you now have in your hands.

Greg's path was like mine in many ways, but this book represents what I believe will be his most significant and lasting contribution in championing the theological renewal of the churches that have a Wesleyan heritage. *Feasting in the Wilderness* is the latest of several books he has written highlighting the people who practiced Wesleyan theology in its early days, the camp meetings that brought that expression of the faith to the general populace, and the core ideas embodied in this theology. I would encourage you to explore his earlier books as well, as together they form a library of exceptional work on these topics. You will not be disappointed. Greg is not only an effective pastor and leader. He is an able historian and author.

I believe this latest book will make a major contribution to theological renewal and church vitality by helping to recover the vital role of the sacrament of Holy Communion in Wesleyan religious practice. My personal observation has been that in too many Methodist parishes the sacraments are relegated to a diminished status in the mind of the congregants because of sporadic practice or a history of anemic teaching regarding what is really the powerful intrinsic dynamic of the Eucharist. This book will correct this reality if read and engaged by both clergy and laity. If so we can regain the central importance Wesley and others gave it in their thinking and practice.

I had personal experience with this in my last appointment, where the first service of worship each Sunday morning was held around tables in the "Fellowship Hall" and included Holy Communion every time we gathered. It was the service that increased most in percentage of attendance while also having within it the widest range of ages who participated. We frequently had teens assisting with the distribution of the elements.

I invite you to join Dr. D. Gregory Van Dussen as he takes us through a journey toward recovering and appreciating what Wesley called a means of grace and a certain way to strengthen and refresh our souls. This, along with the exploration of the historical foundations of the Wesleyan heritage, will bring vitality to your own practice and disciplines of worship.

May we in reading this book make a firm decision to come to the feast which God has given us, that we might again and again have life and have it to the full in our churches and in our personal lives. If we do, God will bring the renewal we so long for and need.

Larry R. Baird
Clarence, NY

Acknowledgements

Many thanks to Marc and Michelle Johnson of Millennium Computers for expert, patient technical assistance. Thanks to Rev. Larry Baird for providing the Foreword. Much appreciation to Elizabeth Lynch for her careful proofreading. Thanks also to Rev. Karen Mc Caffery and congregation of the Indian Falls Global Methodist Church for encouragement along the way, and to Pastor Mc Caffery for the inside photograph, "Wilderness Communion." The books pictured are an 1828 Book of Discipline (which contains the liturgy for the Lord's Supper) and an 1831 Hymnal, both Methodist Episcopal.

Wilderness Communion

Introduction

The lives and times of Methodist circuit riders have long fascinated their spiritual descendants, in North America and wherever else their memory continues to inspire. That fascination nearly always turns to questions. What gave them their determination? How did they achieve such success in growing the churches of their movement? What motivated them to face the struggles, dangers and deprivation inherent in their calling? How did they manage to learn and grow in order to do their work when they were almost constantly traveling and maintaining a daunting schedule and workload?

The answer to all these question and more is found in the presence and power of God, characterized by grace and conveyed by various channels called by John Wesley, means of grace. Of the many examples of those means, which include Scripture and prayer, are the sacraments, and, most relevant to our questions about circuit riders, the one often called simply "the sacrament," the Lord's Supper.

> In the many books written by and about the circuit riders, this sacrament is most often referred to as "the Lord's Supper," but also as "Communion" or "Holy Communion" and, with a frequency I find surprising, "the Eucharist." The word "Lord's" is always capitalized, while the others often appear in lower case. In this book I use capitals for all of them for my own writing, but when quoting a document, I retain the usage of the original author.

The place around which Communion was celebrated and shared was most often called "the Lord's table," rather than "the altar." In the various source documents, those presiding at the

Eucharist were bishops or other ordained ministers, especially "presiding elders." In some Methodist denominations this term remains in use, (or has been restored to use) while in others "district superintendent" has taken its place. In the early days, presiding elders generally led quarterly meetings and were the chief celebrants at their closing Eucharists. Quarterly meetings gathered people from circuits in a presiding elder's district. They were mainly designed for worship and often included baptisms, but also cared for supervisory responsibilities and decision making. They closed with a love feast, at which people shared their testimonies, and the Lord's Supper. When camp meetings exploded onto the scene, quickly becoming the leading form of revival, bishops and presiding elders continued to play important leadership roles, including at the sacrament. Camp meetings became vitally important for Methodists as "extraordinary means of grace."

Some have seen them as so important they eclipsed such traditional means as Holy Communion. However, Communion kept its place as the culminating experience of God's presence and power, even at camp meetings, so that there was actually a new integration of traditional and extraordinary means in the lives of the people.

Presiding elders were critical to the extended organizational network that spread the Methodist message over the far flung territories of Canada and the United States. Situated between the circuits and the bishops, they were the glue that held the connexion together. They were often the ones who made Communion available to the scattered church. Especially on the frontier, their work was hard and the ground they covered was often vast. One of their number, Francis Poythress [c. 1745 – c. 1818] exhausted himself (in 1800) on a district covering fifteen Appalachian circuits. Another, the famous Peter Cartwright [1785-1872], served as a presiding elder in the West for a staggering fifty years.[1]

---

[1] W.P. Strickland, ed. *Sketches of Western Methodism ... by Rev. James B. Finley*. Cincinnati, OH: Methodist Book Concern, for the Author, 1856, 131; W.S. Hooper, ed. Peter Cartwright, *Fifty Years as a Presiding Elder*. Cincinnati, OH: Jenning1s & Graham, 1871.

Of course, the beliefs and actions of the circuit riders did not spring up *de novo*. Those who led the Methodist movement on this continent were very much aware of their connection with John Wesley and others in Britain and Ireland. While Wesley was alive, they corresponded with him, sought his advice, and kept him informed of events on this side of the Atlantic. Long after his passing, they read and reprinted his books and magazines and saw themselves as part of one transatlantic community. They also, quite naturally, developed their own distinctive culture – actually cultures - for they evolved differently in Canada and the States, and even in the various regions within those countries. Still more variety followed with separations here, while other separated bodies were imported by British emigrants. Additional variations came with the Evangelical Association and the United Brethren in Christ, German-American denominations that shared doctrinal and organizational characteristics with "English" Methodists. All this proliferation should not obscure the underlying family resemblances across the movement.

This study includes some of the people and writings that gave Methodism its Wesleyan sacramental identity: John Wesley [1703-1791], the great theologian, evangelist, and organizing genius of the movement; Charles Wesley [1707-1788], also a great theologian, but better known as a prolific hymn writer, and the Irish Bible scholar Adam Clarke [1760-1832]. We will look especially at two of John's sermons, many of John's and, chiefly, Charles' Eucharistic hymns, and two of Clarke's writings on the Lord's Supper. These were foundational to Methodist Eucharistic thought and practice. The Wesleys' ideas remain highly influential to this day. Of special importance is their teaching on real presence, which continued to be a vital part of the experience of early Methodism on this continent.

Finally, we will explore the enduring legacy of these ideas for our own time and their place in ecumenical Christianity. In particular, we will consider the necessary relationship between the Wesleyan theology of grace and the doctrine of real presence. Humanity's hope and destiny in God's new creation rests upon the work of sanctifying grace, which builds upon conversion or justification. The grace-empowered experience of justification in turn follows upon the activity of prevenient grace. One indispensable means of this pattern of grace is the Lord's Supper. The reason the sacrament is so effective in this regard is the powerful presence of Christ, through the Holy Spirit, bringing about human transformation.

The Wesleys contrasted their theology of Eucharistic presence in two directions. They distinguished it from mere memorialism on the one hand, and transubstantiation on the other. Remembrance is, in accordance with Christ's own words, an essential part of the Supper, but not the only part. In the Eucharist we remember Jesus' sacrifice and its purpose. This we share with other Christians, including, of course, memorialists. Real presence recognizes Christ's active involvement in the Holy Meal, transforming us by grace, making us more like himself. While we do not subscribe to a particular theory of presence – in fact we disagree with any teaching that is overly analytical - we stand united with those who recognize him in the breaking of bread. With John Wesley and the early circuit riders, we find that he meets us at the Lord's table, which is one way he leads us on "the way to heaven."[2]

Thus we find ourselves in the company of those who agree on the Lord's presence, but without "putting too fine a point on it" in terms of doctrinal precision. It is important to acknowledge that we have sometimes been more ready to argue the differences than to celebrate our common ground. It is a joy to realize that, in spite of differences, Wesley and the circuit riders stand squarely on that solid, common ground. We share that common ground with many catholic traditions, including Orthodox and Lutherans, though we and they have our own ways of defining what real presence means.

North America provided a hospitable proving ground for Wesley's renewed expression of Christianity. The continent's abundant land was taken, by force and deception, from its indigenous owners, yet the story of cross cultural interaction included many shining examples in which Europeans and First Nations people

---

[2] Albert C. Outler, ed. *The Works of John Wesley*. Nashville, TN: Abingdon, 1984, I:105.)

found deep unity in the Christian gospel – unity so deep it could rival ethnicity as a basis of identity. Many such accounts are included in this study, from both the United States and Canada. Twin emphases of the book are profound spiritual transformation of individuals and reconciliation of divided groups, both made possible by the real presence of Christ in the Eucharist and his genuine involvement in the lives of the people called Methodists. The strange, miraculous capacity to achieve that kind of radical personal and social transformation was rooted in the word of God, which was and remains "alive and active," able to get well beyond humanity's profound and superficial obstacles and divisions to "achieve the purpose for which [he] sent it."[3]

When we juxtapose our thought world with that of the early Methodists, we are inevitably struck by their differences. Yet, dramatic as those differences may be, they cannot override our unity over time. As different as the circuit riders' world is from our own, the center of our worlds remains very much the same. He is "the first and the last, and the living one," "the bread that comes down from heaven and gives life to the world;" the one who "is the same yesterday and today and forever."[4]

---

[3] Hebrews 4:12, NIV; Isaiah 55:11, NIV.
[4] Revelation 1:17&18, ESV; John 6:13, NIV; Hebrews 13:8, NIV.

"When we bless the cup of blessing,
is it not a means of sharing in the blood of Christ?
When we break the bread,
is it not a means of sharing in the body of Christ?"

(I Corinthians 10:16, REB)

"The body of our Lord Jesus Christ, which was given for thee, Preserve thy body and soul unto everlasting life:
Take and eat this in remembrance that Christ died for thee, feed on him in thy heart by faith with thanksgiving.

"The blood of our Lord Jesus Christ, which was shed for thee, Preserve thy body and soul unto everlasting life:
Drink this in remembrance that Christ's blood was shed for thee and be thankful.
(1662 Book of Common Prayer)

Chapter 1

John Wesley and Adam Clarke on the Importance of Eucharistic Worship

"It is very meet, right and our bounden duty,
that we should at all times, and in all places,
give thanks unto thee, O Lord, Holy Father, Almighty,
Everlasting God."[1]

John Wesley [1703-1791] wondered why any Christian would turn away from the blessings Jesus gave us in the Lord's Supper. Holy Communion held an important place in Methodist worship from the beginning of Wesley' revival. He believed it was the duty, as well as the blessing, of everyone in his movement to take part in this sacrament as often as possible. Hoards of his early converts crowded parish churches, seeking to receive this means of grace. He and his brother Charles [1707-1788] supplied Eucharistic hymns both to give voice to people's worship and to remind them of the depth and breadth of meaning in this sacrament. In the introduction to his adaptation of *The Book of Common Prayer* for the newly independent Methodist Episcopal Church in America, Wesley "advise[d] the elders to administer the supper of the

---

[1] 1662 Book of Common Prayer.

Lord on every Lord's day."[2] His advice would raise obvious logistical difficulties, especially in the beginning, but it made very clear Wesley's vision and intent for his movement and the high place he gave to this sacrament in the life of the Church.

The foundation for all this was in Scripture and the teaching and practice of the "primitive church." Wesley began his sermon on "The Duty of Constant Communion" with Jesus' command, "Do this in remembrance of me." He made it clear from the start that, for Christians, participation in this sacrament was not optional. He also wondered why anyone would think of Holy Communion as anything but a great blessing, to be received not reluctantly but gratefully, as often as possible. Wesley acknowledges that "One reason why many neglect it is, they are so much afraid of 'eating and drinking unworthily' that they never think how much greater the danger is when do not eat or drink at all."[3] This mistaken view of the matter is based on a misunderstanding of I Corinthians 11: 29. Paul's intent here is not to build a wall around the Eucharist, one that only the worthy can scale. It is rather to make sure people are celebrating in the way Jesus intended. Wesley's sermon makes two major points, both of which underscore the significance of the sacrament. First, the Lord's Supper is far from being a trivial matter:

> "…all Christians [were] obliged to receive those signs of Christ's body and blood. Here therefore the bread and wine are commanded to be received, in remembrance of his death, to the end of the world. Observe, too, that this command was given by our Lord when he was just laying down his life for our sakes. They are therefore, as it were, his dying words to all his followers. (John Wesley. "Constant Communion", 429.)

But Wesley not only wanted to impress upon his readers the authority and awesome profundity of Holy Communion; he also

---

[2] Letter "To Dr. Coke, Mr. Asbury, and our Brethren in North-America." Jonathan H, Johnson, ed. *John Wesley's The Book of Common Prayer (The Sunday Service of the Methodists of North America,* [orig. 1784]. Marshfield, WI: Furocious Studios, 2018, xvi.

[3] John Wesley. "The Duty of Constant Communion." Albert C. Outler, ed. *The Works of John Wesley*. Nashville, TN: Abingdon, 1986, 3: 428.

wanted them to grasp the reason for Jesus' command. This repeated celebration was designed not to be a burden, nor a fortress to be defended, but a treasured spiritual bounty. Thus, "A second reason why every Christian should do this as often as he can is because the benefits of doing so are so great to all that do it in obedience to him, namely, the forgiveness of our past sins and the present strengthening and refreshing of our souls." Here was freedom from the shackles of the past and power for a very different kind of future: a means of grace.

His reasoning comes from the connection he makes between his Eucharistic theology and his overarching theology of salvation. In both cases, everything comes down to grace. Since the Eucharist is a means of grace, it is not a reward to be earned by accumulating "worthiness," points, but a gift to be graciously accepted. The grace-filled Eucharist is a remedy for sin, not recognition of self-generated righteousness. It is power for the path of life (Psalm 16: 11, NIV); spiritual fuel on the road of sanctification, relevant to every stage of the journey. The Lord's Supper brings us the riches of the whole panorama of grace, "grace upon grace," prevenient, justifying, and sanctifying. Two major themes emerge from John and Charles [1707-88] Wesley's hymns. One is rooted in a name given to Jesus before his birth and surfaces again in promises he made to his disciples. In Matthew 1;23 we read the familiar Christmas promise, "the virgin will conceive and give birth to a son, and they will call him Immanuel [Emmanuel] (which means "God with us" John 1:16, ESV; Matthew 1:23, NIV). John's Gospel makes Jesus' identity very clear:

> In the beginning was the Word, and the Word was with God, and the Word was God. He was with God in the beginning. Through him all things were made; without him nothing was made that has been made. In him was life, and that life was the light of all mankind. The light shines in the darkness, and the darkness has not overcome it.[4]

---

[4] John 1:1-5, NIV.

Jesus not only serves God as a messenger or spokesperson. He is "the radiance of God's glory and the exact representation of his being." (Hebrews 1:3, NIV.) Similarly, we read in Colossians,

> The Son is the image of the invisible God, the firstborn over all creation. For in him all things were created: things in heaven and on earth, visible and invisible ... all things have been created through him and for him. He is before all things, and in him all things hold together. And he is the head of the body, the church; he is the beginning and the firstborn from among the dead, so that in everything he might have the supremacy. For God was pleased to have all his fullness dwell in him....[5]

At the Last Supper, Jesus extended the significance of Israel's sacred memory that was already central to the feast of Passover, to establish in the Eucharist the universal commemoration of his sacrifice on our behalf. As he spoke and acted out the new words and actions he was adding to the ceremony, he told his apostles and all who would follow them, "Do this in remembrance of me." (Luke 21:19, NIV.) In reenacting the drama of that night, we would discover and receive his presence, continuing through the ages, until that meal finds its fulfillment in sharing the heavenly banquet. Until then, we could encounter him much as his two disciples did when he broke bread with them at the end of their walk to Emmaus.

> When he was at the table with them, he took bread, gave thanks, broke it and began to give it to them. Then their eyes were opened and they recognized him, and he disappeared from their sight. They asked each other, "Were not our hearts burning within us while he talked with us on the road and opened the Scriptures to us?"
>
> They got up and returned at once to Jerusalem. There they found the Eleven and those with them, assembled with them and saying, "It is true! The Lord has risen and has appeared to Simon." Then the two told what had happened on the way, and how Jesus was recognized by them when he broke the bread[6].

---

[5] Colossians 1:15-19, NIV.
[6] Luke 24:30-35, NIV.

Not surprisingly, early Methodist preachers sometimes related their own Communion experiences to this encounter on the road to Emmaus.

Jesus' purpose in instituting the sacrament, was, first of all, to convey his promise to remain with us forever. He did this specifically in terms of our memory, our prayer and worship, and through the ongoing presence and power of the Holy Spirit. Regarding prayer, he said, "For where two or three are gathered in my name, there am I among them." (Matthew 18;20, ESV.) To empower the Church for its mission, he said, "Surely I will be with you always, to the very end of the age." (Matthew 28:20, NIV.) In his physical absence he promised that the Holy Spirit would teach and strengthen them. (John 14:5-17.)

The second purpose is Jesus' mission to make us, by grace, like himself, and to take us to be where he is. (II Corinthians 3:17&18; II Peter 1:4; I John 3:2; John 14:3.) Both of these themes are partly, yet abundantly fulfilled by his presence in the meal he gave us. The theology and experience of Holy Communion both paralleled and embodied Wesley's way of salvation, the panorama of grace. It was far from being either a means of generalized grace, blanketing life with comfort and inspiration, or a peculiar sort of grace, to be drawn upon only for certain specified occasions. Instead, it is a conduit of prevenient, justifying, and sanctifying grace, poured out upon us, and through us, giving life to the world. Eucharistic grace flows from Christ's real, actual presence in the meal he so generously gave us, to sustain, guide, and empower us on the road of life. In this holy meal the body of Christ is renewed and refreshed for its mission. Its grace is relevant to every stage in our lives, awakening us to new awareness of our sin and of his seeking (prevenient grace, conviction) bringing us to repentance and a radical new beginning (justifying grace, new birth, new creation), and opening up endless new vistas, leading us into an eternity of spiritual growth (sanctifying grace, Christian perfection, becoming "like him" [I John 3:2, NIV] Wesley called all of this "the way to heaven."[7]

---

[7] Albert C. Outler, ed. *The Works of John Wesley*. Nashville, TN: Abingdon, 1984, 1:105.

Communion, as the word suggests, unites us anew, repeatedly, throughout our lives, with the One who calls us and draws us together, and with our fellow pilgrims, who share the same journey, traveling toward the same destination. In Communion we renew our identity as branches of the same vine and members together of the body of Christ. For "in Christ, we, though many, form one body, and each member belongs to all the others." (John 15:5; Romans 12:5, NIV) The circle we are part of is not closed: as once it opened to receive us, again and again it opens to new partakers, at one stage or another, in the same grace we have known. We learn from each other and help each other to navigate the sometimes treacherous, always difficult route he shows us, even the seemingly final transition called death. We also celebrate the joys and hard won victories along the way, experiences that point to, and mysteriously participate in, the ultimate celebration in heaven. (Romans 12:15)

As we have seen, John Wesley's sermon on "The Duty of Constant Communion" takes as its starting point Jesus' command at the Last Supper, "Do this in remembrance of me."(Luke 22:19, NIV), He attributes a pattern of "neglect" on the part of many in his day to a misunderstanding of Paul's warning in I Corinthians about taking Communion in an unworthy manner, and by doing so, placing themselves under God's judgment. (I Corinthians 11:29) Taking unworthiness in a broader sense, Wesley points out that our human sinfulness is precisely the reason we need to receive the sacrament. Access to the Lord's table is not something to be won by human effort as a kind of reward for good behavior or spiritual achievement, but rather a gift bestowed, to be received with gratitude.

Wesley' sermon emphasizes two major points, both reasons for partaking of the Eucharist and doing so as often as possible. The first is obedience to Jesus' command.

...it is the duty of every Christian to receive the Lord's Supper as often as he can.

> The first reason why it is the duty of every Christian so to do is because it is a plain command of Christ. ... Here therefore the bread and wine are commanded to be received, in remembrance

of his death, to the end of the world. Observe, too, that this command was given by our Lord when he was just laying down his life for our sakes. They are therefore, as it were, his dying words to his followers.

This is not merely an acknowledgement of authority, but a grateful recognition of an incalculable gift and blessing. Thus, "A second reason why every Christian should do this as often as he can is because the benefits of doing it are so great to all that do it in obedience to him, namely, the forgiveness of our past sins and the present strengthening and refreshing of our souls."[8]

The Lord's Supper "fits" into Wesley's theology of salvation because, as a means of grace, it provides resources needed at every stage of the journey of faith. Prevenient grace seeks us out before we are even aware of our need, awakens us to that need, convicts us of our sin and points the way to our salvation. (Romans 5:6-8) Justifying grace leads us through repentance and forgiveness to a place of rejoicing as we begin a radically new life. (Romans 5:1-2; II Corinthians 5:17) Sanctifying grace empowers our transformation into the likeness of Christ. (II Corinthians 3:18; I John 3:2) Holy Communion is, so to speak, a delivery system, for the panoply of God's grace, exemplifying the "grace upon grace" which "we all have received." (John 1:16, ESV)

> Whoever therefore does not receive, but goes from the holy table when all things are prepared, either does not understand his duty or does not care for the dying command of his Saviour, the forgiveness of his sins, the strengthening of his soul, and the refreshing it with the hope of glory. (John Wesley. "Constant Communion." 429.)

Wesley uses the classic description of the bread and wine as "outward signs of the inward grace." He argues that constant Communion is God's way for us to be "eternally happy" while "all who do not [accept the invitation/command and receive its benefits] shall be eternally miserable." Obedience to Christ's commandment leads to our destination in glory, while one who neglects this opportunity "will have no place in the kingdom of

---

[8] John Wesley. "Constant Communion."3: 428-429.

heaven." While this may seem an overly strict case of rule keeping or legalism, Wesley sees it as a very generous way God seeks our well-being.

> As God ... knew there was but one way for man to be happy like himself, namely, by being like him in holiness; as he knew we could do nothing toward this of ourselves, he has given us certain means of obtaining his help. One of these is the Lord's Supper, which of his infinite mercy he hath given us for this very end: that through this means we may be assisted to attain those blessings which he hath prepared for us, that we may obtain holiness on earth and everlasting glory in heaven[9].

To say that one is unworthy to receive this gift, and the blessings it conveys, is both obvious and completely beside the point, for worthiness belongs only to the Giver, and he is the one who offers the gift and commands us to receive it. To claim our unworthiness as the reason for resisting the command is to place a completely unwarranted condition upon the gift, as well as to deprive ourselves of the blessings it contains.

To cite unworthiness as a reason to commune less often makes no sense, either, because the same unworthiness applies to infrequent Communion as much as frequent or constant Communion. The excuse of unworthiness "is not so properly an objection against constantly communicating as against communicating at all."

Wesley also argues against limiting participation on the ground that constant Communion might lessen its meaning or power by becoming too ordinary. He denies that this is necessarily the case and questions its apparent import in view of the reasons supporting the practice.[10]

Wesley elaborated further the importance he saw in the Eucharist in another sermon, "The Means of Grace." He begins by taking us back to the earliest Church, when there was no confusion about the Sacrament actually conveying grace.

Are there, under the Christian dispensation, any 'means' or-

---

[9] John Wesley. "Constant Communion." 431-432.
[10] John Wesley. "Constant Communion." 435-437.

dained of God as the usual channels of his grace? This question could never have been proposed in the apostolical church unless by one who openly avowed himself to be a heathen, the whole body of Christians being agreed that Christ had ordained certain outward means for conveying his grace into the souls of men. Their constant practice set this beyond all dispute; for so long as "all that believed were together, and had all things common," "they continued steadfastly in the teaching of the apostles, and in the breaking of bread, and in prayers."[11]

But over time, this original understanding became obscured, as did the flow of grace through this channel. Holy Communion could still produce fruit in the lives of God's people, and would do so again in a renewed Church. So it had been through the ages, whenever there were those "experimentally acquainted with true, inward religion," and not merely "the form of godliness."[12]

Wesley's clarity on "means of grace" will help us discern where and when the Sacraments have functioned as intended. He wrote, "By 'means of grace' I understand outward signs, words, or actions ordained of God, and appointed for this end – to be the *ordinary* channels whereby he might convey to men preventing [prevenient], justifying, or sanctifying grace."[13]

Wesley's list of these means of grace includes, but goes beyond sacraments, but sacraments are important examples. He mentions the Church of England's designation of a sacrament as "an outward sign of an inward *grace,* and a *means* whereby we receive the same." Among these he describes "receiving the Lord's Supper, eating bread and drinking wine in remembrance of him [Christ]," which is one of the "ordinary channels of conveying his grace to the souls of men." It is the effective transmission of grace that gives value to the means of delivery, "consequently ... these means, when separated from the end, are less than nothing, and vanity...." If they do not accomplish their purpose; "if they do not actually conduce to the knowledge and love of God they are

---

[11] John Wesley. "The Means of Grace," Albert C. Outler, ed. The Works of John Wesley. Nashville, TN: Abingdon, 1984, 1: 378; Acts 2:42.

[12] John Wesley. "Means of Grace." 1: 379; II Timothy 3:5, NIV.

[13] John Wesley. "Means of Grace." 1:381.

not acceptable in his sight...." In other words, "all outward means whatever, if separate from the Spirit of God, cannot profit at all.... (John Wesley. "Means of Grace." 1:381-382.)

Reciting the words and acting out the form of Holy Communion can never be a substitute for the grace it is intended to convey, but repeating it as originally intended is one God-given way of making ourselves available to receive his grace. It is a way to live the words of Jesus when he promised his followers that if they would truly seek God, they would surely find him (Jeremiah 29:13; Matthew 7:7). Here is the way, if we devote ourselves to it throughout our lives, we can hope to "enter into his kingdom." This promise of the kingdom, made over and over again in Jesus' parables, Wesley applies to all the means of grace, including the Eucharist, about which he said,

> All who desire an increase of the grace of God are to wait for it in partaking of the Lord's Supper. For this also is a direction himself hath given [in I Corinthians 10:16] ...
>
> Is not the eating of that bread, and the drinking of that cup, the outward, visible means whereby God conveys into our souls all that spiritual grace, that righteousness, and peace, and joy in the Holy Ghost, which were purchased by the body of Christ once broken and the blood of Christ once shed for us? Let all, therefore, who truly desire the grace of God, eat of that bread and drink of that cup.[14]

Wesley uses an interesting expression to tell us what happens when we partake of the Lord's Supper: when we approach the Sacrament in the way Christ intended, trusting his promise and relying on his grace, we can trust "that he will meet [us] there.... I do expect that he will fulfil his Word, that he will meet and bless me in this way." We will see this same expression again in the writing of circuit riders. What this cannot possibly mean is that when we commune there is no one there! No one to "meet" at the altar; no one to offer grace. In other words, it cannot mean that Christ is not really present.[15]

---

[14] John Wesley. "Means of Grace," 1:384 - 390.
[15] John Wesley. "The Means of Grace," 1: 391.

At the same time, Wesley is very clear, both that God is not limited to any particular means, and that there is nothing automatic in their effectiveness.

> As to the manner of using them, whereon indeed it wholly depends whether they should convey ay grace at all to the user, it behoves us, first, always to retain a lively sense that God is above all means. Have a care therefore of limiting the Almighty. He doth whatsoever and whensoever it pleaseth him. He can convey his grace, either in or out of any of the means which he hath appointed.

> ... in using all means, seek God alone. In and through every outward thing look singly to the power of his Spirit and the merits of his Son. Beware you do not stick in the work itself; if you do, it is all lost labour. Nothing short of God can satisfy your soul. Therefore eye him in all, through all, and above all.

> Remember also to use all means as means; as ordained, not for their own sake, but in order to the renewal of your soul in righteousness and true holiness.[16]

Wesley is here describing the availability of power, the power of grace, the power of the Holy Spirit, never to be taken for granted and never separated from its divine source. His great care in avoiding misunderstanding and misuse of the means of grace clarifies, without weakening, the blessings God intended them to convey, at every step of our journey along "the way to heaven." The means he describes are God's ways of providing spiritual resources we all need for that journey.[17]

At the very least, Wesley's sermons highlight the enduring importance of the Lord's Supper to the Methodist movement and to Christianity as a whole. That much of his position is echoed by the great Methodist Bible scholar Adam Clarke [1760-1832], though Clarke has a very different view of the ideal frequency for receiving Communion.

---

[16] John Wesley. "Means of Grace," 1:395 -397.
[17] John Wesley, Preface to Sermons, Outler. *Works of John Wesley.* 1:105.

.In 1808, Clarke published *A Discourse on the Nature and Design of the Eucharist, or Sacrament of the Lord's Supper,* in which he emphasized remembrance in discussing the meaning of the sacrament: "The holy eucharist I consider a rite designed by God to keep up a continual remembrance of the doctrine of the ATONEMENT." (p. 4.) Among the things remembered were the context of the Passover and the words and actions with which Jesus led the thoughts and prayers of those who gathered to commemorate and celebrate the event. But important as was the traditional Passover, their supper would be much more than recalling and giving thanks for the historic liberation of the Jewish people from slavery in Egypt. Jesus was adding new meanings, connected to Passover but extending well beyond it. Like the Passover, this new mystery was to be celebrated far into the future, but unlike it, they would be remembering his sacrifice, which would set us free not from Egyptian slavery, but from the much larger captors, sin and death. "The last enemy to be destroyed is death."[18]

> Among the ordinances prescribed by the gospel, that commonly called the sacrament of the Lord's supper has ever held a distinguished place; and the church of Christ in all ages, has represented the due religious celebration of it as a duty incumbent on every soul that professed faith in Jesus Christ, and sought for salvation through his blood alone. Hence it was ever held in the highest estimation and reverence; and the great High Priest of his church showed, by more than ordinary influences of his blessed Spirit on the souls of the faithful, that they had not mistaken his meaning, nor believed in vain; that, while by eating of that bread, and drinking of that cup, they endeavored to show forth his death, and realize the benefits to be derived from it.[19]

Clarke denounces in the strongest terms the medieval doctrine of transubstantiation and believes it must yield to earlier teaching, for example that of Justin Martyr, in which the Eucharistic sacrifice was "a type of Christ crucified for the sins of the world," rather than an actual sacrifice of the literal body and blood of

---

[18] I Corinthians 15:26, NIV.

[19] Adam Clarke. A Discourse on the Nature and Design of the Lord's Supper. New York, NY: G. Lane & P.P. Sandford, 1842, 4; 31-32.

Christ. His rejection of transubstantiation agrees with the Articles of Religion of The Book of Common Prayer and specifically article 18 in Wesley's version. It also places Clarke in a doctrinal position similar to many other Protestants. However, what it does not do is to identify Methodists (or Anglicans, for that matter) as mere memorialists. Instead, by the same BCP standard, Methodism has found Christ to be really present, "after an heavenly and spiritual manner. And the means whereby the body of Christ is received and eaten in the supper, is faith."[20]

The Supper of the Lord is one place where Jesus fulfills his promise to be "with [us] always, to the very end of the age." (Matthew 28:20, NIV) What Clarke, Methodism, and The Book of Common Prayer tell us is that Communion is an effective means of bringing us the transforming power of grace.

A vital part of that transformation, for Clarke, is "that all sin might be destroyed" and "that truth, the law of righteousness and true holiness, might regulate and guide all the actions of life." This effect goes well beyond a mere transaction or a temporary disposal of particular sins, which are, after all, only symptoms of a deeper and larger "bent to sinning."[21]

Jesus also refers to the wine of the Last Supper as, "my blood of the covenant, which is poured out for many for the forgiveness of sins." (Matthew 26:28, NIV) Clarke says, "this holy eucharist was, in a great measure, copied from the paschal feast and was intended to supply its place" in our redemption. Again, instead of being merely a limited transaction, perhaps one of enlightened self-interest, Communion points to and participates in a thoroughgoing change in our relationship with God. The Eucharist celebrates and facilitates a change of character, and acts out our being set free from bondage to sin and death. As a covenant, it proclaims God's faithfulness to his part in this promised transformation. The "blood of the covenant" signifies "the grand plan

---

[20] Jonathan H. Johnson, ed. *John Wesley's The Book of Common Prayer. (The Sunday Service of the Methodists of North America,* orig. 1784), Marshfield, WI, Furocious Studios, 2018, 278.

[21] Charles Wesley. "Love Divine, All Loves Excelling." *Our Great Redeemer's Praise*. Franklin, TN: Seedbed, 2022, #88, v.2.)

of agreement, or reconciliation, which God was now establishing between himself and mankind," which overcomes the separation caused by sin. Since that is the nature and intent of the sacrament, "Those, therefore, who reject the Lord's Supper, sin against their own mercies, and treat their Maker with the basest ingratitude."[22]

Part of the reason for Jesus' presiding at the Last Supper, and our carrying out his intention by repeating it for new generations of partakers, is to offer blessing and thanksgiving for all that God has done for us. Our entire lives should be lived this way, but the appropriateness is magnified in this feast of our salvation, which focuses our thoughts on the price Jesus paid and the victory he won. The breaking of the bread is a sign of his sacrifice, a vivid liturgical action and reminder of the violence willingly endured for us. The bread and wine, for Clark, signify or represent, without literally being transformed into, the body and blood of Christ.[23] One of the most hope-filled words of Jesus during the Last Supper causes us to gaze into the future to the ultimate shared meal of heaven, where there will be new wine, a sign of a new reality, "a sign of and pledge to genuine Christians of the felicity they shall enjoy with Christ in the kingdom of glory." Here we are reminded of one of the essential ingredients in worship: fellowship, fellowship of the purest kind. (Matthew 26:29; Acts 2:42; I John 1:3)

As the term koinonia means not only communion or fellowship but also participation, "it thereby signifies that the faithful partakers had thereby fellowship or communion with the Lord Jesus, being made partakers of the benefits of his passion and death: so that as truly as their bodies were made partakers of, and were nourished by, the bread and wine, so truly were their souls made partakers of the grace, mind, and spirit of the Lord Jesus," so that "they dwelt in God, and God in them; were one with God, and God with them."[24]

Here we see one more reason, the supreme reason, to give thanks and rejoice. Clarke quotes John Chrysostom: "Besides this ... those tremendous mysteries, replenished with abundance

---

[22] Clarke. *Lord's Supper.* 55; 48-49; 82; 89.

[23] Clarke, *Lord's Supper,* 94; 56; 59.

[24] Clarke. *Lord's Supper.* 101- 102.

of salvation, which we celebrate in every congregation, are called the EUCHARIST [thanksgiving], because they are the memorial of many benefits, and pour out the SUM of God's providence, and prepare us to give thanks in all things." In the sacrifice commemorated here, "God had given us all possible blessings, and therefore ... the eucharist, by which these things were called to remembrance, is a means of replenishing faithful believers with the plenitude of salvation, by which they are enabled to walk uprightly before God and give him due thanks for his unspeakable gift." Clarke defines the sacrifice that made all this possible as "God offering himself entirely, in and through Christ, not only to every true believer, but to every penitent," and requiring a like response from all who share the mystery.[25] Here the perfection of the sacrament mirrors the sanctification of the partaker.

Given the profound significance and seriousness involved in taking Communion, is it any wonder, in ancient times or modern, that many would resist participating by saying, "But I am not worthy?" Here is Clarke's reply (echoing Wesley): "And who is? There is not a saint upon earth, or an archangel in heaven, who is worthy to sit down at the table of the Lord." (Clarke. *Lord's Supper* 122.) Clarke goes on to say, like Wesley, that the point at issue here is the purpose of the sacrament as a means of grace. The partaker does not come already worthy, but seeking grace in order to be set free from the burden of sin – ultimately completely free of all sin – and to access the sanctifying grace that transforms. To come in that manner, seeking forgiveness and transformation, is to participate worthily.

When it comes to the frequency of receiving Holy Communion, Clarke differs from Wesley. Where Wesley encouraged people to commune as often as possible, Clarke believed that monthly Communion offered appropriate intervals for a proper recognition of the meaning of the event, and that, "Every soul, who wishes not to abjure his right to the benefits of Christ's passion and death, should make it a point with God and his conscience to partake of this ordinance at least four or six times in the year." Even so, Clarke is unwavering in his belief in the profound im-

---

[25] Clarke. Lord's Supper. 95; 99.

portance of the Eucharist, as where he writes, "He who does not receive the holy sacrament, in reference to the atonement made by the passion and death of Christ, shall also bear his own sin. Let no soul trifle here: if a man believe that the due observance of this ordinance is divinely authorized, he cannot refrain from its celebration and be guiltless." In his view, it is possible to commune too frequently, as well as too seldom.

> Those who receive it only once in a year, cannot sufficiently feel the weight of the divine command. The intervals between the times of celebration are so long, that it is almost impossible to keep up the commemoration of the great facts shadowed forth by this ordinance. On the other hand, those who take it daily, or once in the week, become too much familiarized with it, properly to respect its nature and design.[26]

Adam Clarke's *Christian Theology* also contains a chapter on the Lord's Supper. He begins with a combative characterization of Roman Catholic treatment of the Eucharist. In his view, Catholics "pretend to transmute, by a kind of spiritual incantation, the bread and wine into the real body and blood of Jesus Christ – a measure, the grossest in folly, and most stupid in nonsense, to which God in judgment ever abandoned the fallen spirit of man." Even so, Clarke reveals the high regard in which he holds this Sacrament, which he calls "the most important and divine of all God's ordinances." While he derides the way Catholic celebrants handle the elements, he goes to some length to lay out the proper, reverential way the elements should be treated. No doubt the virulence of some of his comments owes much to the deep cultural and political divide between Europe's Protestants and Catholics in his day, which was particularly strong in Ireland and Britain.[27]

Clarke emphasizes the remembrance called for in Holy Communion and its relationship to the symbols of bread and wine, but also the spiritual benefits of Jesus' atonement. He calls upon ministers to refuse admission to the Lord's table those he describes as "disreputable and iniquitous guests." In his own color-

---

[26] Clarke. Lord's Supper, 131 – 133.
[27] Adam Clarke. *Christian Theology*. Salem, OH: H.E. Schmul, 1967, 257.

ful language, he asks, "For can it be expected that God will manifest his approbation we the pale of his sanctuary is broken down; and the beasts of the forest introduced into the holy of holies!"[28] The whole matter of grounds for exclusion from Holy Communion continued to trouble Methodists who were concerned to guard the integrity of the sacrament.

In an interesting pastoral sidelight, Clarke includes this observation to illustrate negligence toward the Sacrament:

> Scarcely anything is more unbecoming than to have the majority of communicants, as soon as they have received, posting out of the church or chapel; so that at the conclusion of the ordinance very few are found to join together in a general thanksgiving to God for the benefits conferred by the passion and death of Christ by means of this blessed ordinance.[29]

So it is clear that the Lord's Supper mattered a great deal to John Wesley, the founder of the movement, and to Adam Clarke, its chief Biblical scholar. Also important is the extensive body of Eucharistic hymns written by John and Charles Wesley, which give us a fuller picture of the sacrament's meaning as they handed it on to the Methodists of North America. Of special interest is the interactive connection between their Eucharistic theology and their comprehensive theology of grace.

---

[28] Clarke. *Christian Theology*. 269.
[29] Clarke. Christian Theology. 262.

Chapter 2

Eucharist and Sanctification in the Hymns of John and Charles Wesley

"To find thy real presence there, And all thy fullness gain."[1]

Richard Heitzenrater has this to say about the place of Charles Wesley and his hymns in the Methodist movement:

> Charles's hymns came to represent the popular form of Wesleyan theology; the eighteenth-century revival was to a great extent borne on the wings of Charles' poetry. Charles' hymns not only helped form the texture of the Methodist mind but also, perhaps more importantly, set the temper of the Methodist spirit. (Richard P. Heitzenrater, Foreword, S.T. Kimbrough, Jr. Lost in Wonder: Charles Wesley, the Meaning of His Hymns Today. Nashville, TN: Upper Room, 1987, 11-12.)

S.T. Kimbrough describes the extensive background Charles, much like his brother (though Charles was by far the more prolific hymn writer), brought to his writing: "Wesley was a master of words and was steeped in a strong classical educational tradition which gave him facility in Latin and biblical languages, and a firm foundation in history, theology, and literature." This was a background Charles shared with John and other family members, which served as a deep well from which to draw in his own writing. (Kimbrough. *Lost in Wonder*, 17.) One dimension of this rich

---

[1] Hymns on the Lord's Supper

background that has attracted scholarly attention is the relationship of the Wesleys' thought to that of Eastern Orthodoxy. This historical and theological connection is very strong in Charles hymns and the spirituality behind them.[2]

A major block of Wesley's hymns deals with Eucharistic theology and spirituality. Ernest Rattenbury calls our attention to a line that may serve as an invitation to this theme

> Jesu, dear, redeeming Lord,
> Magnify thy dying word,
> In thine ordinance appear,
> Come, and meet thy followers here.
> In the rite Thou hast enjoin'd,
> Let us now our Saviour find....
> (John and Charles Wesley. Hymns on the Lord's Supper. London: J. Kershaw, 1825, #33; Rattenbury. Eucharistic Hymns, 30.)

The expression, "Come, and meet thy followers here." resembles John Wesley's reference to meeting the Lord in his Supper. The divine-human synergy involved in such meeting is clear in this verse:

> ...The prayer, the fast, the word conveys,
> When mix'd with faith, thy life to me;
> In all the channels of thy grace,
> I still have fellowship with Thee,
> But chiefly here my soul is fed,
> With fulness of immortal bread.... (HLS 54.)

Rattenbury points out "The objective character of the Presence and the subjective Faith needed for its realization" in another hymn:

---

[2] S.T. Kimbrough, Jr., ed. *Orthodox and Wesleyan Spirituality*. Crestwood, NY: St Vladimir's Seminary Press, 2002, especially essays on holiness, 59-126, including Petros Vassiliadis, "Holiness in the Perspective of Eucharistic Theology," 101-116, and "Other Eastern Sources and Charles Wesley," 205-263; Kallistos of Diokleia & Ruediger Minor, eds. Holy Synod of the Ecumenical Patriarchate & World Methodist Council. *Orthodox and Methodists*. Undated Pamphlet.

...Great is thy faithfulness and love,
Thine ordinance can never prove
Of none effect and vain,
Only do Thou my heart prepare,
To find thy real presence there,
And all thy fullness gain. (HLS 66; Rattenbury. Eucharistic Hymns, 37)

Another hymn addresses the matter of real presence, saying,

...We come with confidence to find
Thy special presence here.
His presence makes the feast. .... (HLS 81.)

Again we find a clear indication that something far beyond memory is happening in this meal. "Wesley could not think of the Lord's Supper as only a memorial, a drama in the mind, a 'vivid preaching' of a past event. Rather, in the sacrament believers encounter the living Christ."[3]

Chiefly here my soul is fed
With Fullness of immortal Bread. (HLS 54.)

The "how" of the delivery of Christ's real presence must remain a mystery:

How the Bread his Flesh imparts,
How the Wine transmits his Blood,
Fills his faithful People's Hearts
With all the Life of God! (HLS 57.)

In yet another hymn, we see again the necessary acceptance of mystery and a reference to the Supper as both "figure and means of saving grace:" Here also the sacred meal anticipates the heavenly banquet yet to come:

Author of our salvation, Thee,
With lowly thankful hearts we praise;
Author of this great mystery,
Figure and means of saving grace.

---

[3] Daniel B. Stevick. *The Altar's Fire: Charles Wesley's Hymns on the Lord's Supper (etc.)*. Werrington, UK: Epworth, 2004, 89.

...
We see the blood that seals our peace,
Thy pard'ning mercy we receive:
The bread doth visibly express
The strength through which our spirits live

Our spirits drink a fresh supply,
And eat the bread so freely given;
Till borne on eagles' wings we fly,
And banquet with our Lord in heaven. (HLS 28.)

Kimbrough and Mcintyre draw an important connection between this hymn and #54. Verse 3 is drawn from II Peter 1:4 ("... through them you may participate in the divine nature, having escaped the corruption in the world caused by evil desires." (NIV), a Scripture vital to sanctification theology. Its placement here joins sanctification inseparably with the Eucharist:

... Saviour, thou didst the mystery give
that I thy nature might partake.
Thou bidst me outward signs receive,
one with thyself my soul to make,
my body, soul and spirit join,
inseparably one with thine.... (HLS 54; S.T. Kimbrough & Dean B. McIntyre, eds. A Theology of the Sacraments, Interpreted by John and Charles Wesley. Eugene, OR: Resource, 2021, 39.)

This emphasis on the element of mystery recognizes a necessary humility regarding presence, and the impossibility of coming up with an adequate explanation. A further question is whether there is a need to explain such a mystery:

... I cannot the Way decry,
Need not know the mystery,
Only this I know that I
Was blind, and now I see.... [HLS 59.]

"He [Charles Wesley] no more doubts the fact than he understands the mystery. He is not so foolish as to try to answer the question,"

O the depth of love divine,
the unfathomable grace!

Who shall say how Bread and Wine
God into man conveys.
How the bread his flesh imparts;
How the wine transmits his blood,
Fills his faithful people's hearts
With all the Life of GOD?

Sure and real is the Grace,
The manner be unknown. (Rattenbury. Eucharistic Hymns, 43; HLS 57; Ole Borgen. John Wesley on the Sacraments. Nashville, TN: Abingdon, 65-66.)

"Wesley sees the sacrament as a sign which shows Christ's body and blood, but it is an effectual sign – a sign that enacts what it signifies, a bestowal of God's mercy and strength. The blood imparts pardon, the bread gives sustenance."[4] It is the Spirit who transforms otherwise ordinary elements into life giving signs in this verse that echoes the epiclesis of the Eucharistic prayer:

Come, Holy Ghost, thine influence shed
And realize the sign,
Thy life infuse into the bread,
Thy power into the wine.

Effectual let the tokens prove,
And make by heavenly art
Fit channels to convey thy love
To every faithful heart. (HLS 72)

Still another example rejects any interpretation that falls short of the powerful presence of Christ:

Ah tell us no more,
he spirit and power
Of Jesus our God
Is not to be found in this life-giving food! ....
(HLS 92.)

"Repeatedly and in various ways, Wesley affirms that Christ is truly present, met and received in the sacrament."[5] The hymns

---

[4] Stevick. *Altar's Fire*, 89.
[5] Stevick. *Altar's Fire*, 91.

continue to express the importance of real presence, as in these lines:

> ... We need not now go up to heaven
> To bring the long-sought Saviour down.
> Thou art to all already given:
> Thou dost e'en now thy banquet crown,
> To every faithful soul appear,
> And show thy real presence here. (HLS 116.)

"Jesus who once met his disciples and spoke and ate, is asked to speak the 'gospel-word' again, to break the bread, to open his followers eyes, and their hearts to see and know him, to talk with them until their hearts burn within them."[6] The Emmaus reference appears in this somewhat familiar hymn:

> O Thou who this mysterious bread
> Didst in Emmaus break,
> Return herewith our souls to feed
> And to thy followers speak.... (HLS 29.)

Once again, two related principles and realities that stand out in the Wesley hymns are sanctification and Eucharistic presence. Sanctification is the goal and purpose of Christ's incarnation and rescue mission in this world – God's new creation, our transformation into his likeness by the power of the Holy Spirit (II Corinthians 5:17; 3:18). Christ's Eucharistic presence, is a central resource for making this transformation a reality – a means of grace. In the incarnation, God became like us, so that we could, by grace, become like him (Philippians 2:3-11; 3:21; II Peter 1:4; I John 3:2). All of this is one way of fulfilling Jesus' promise in the Great Commission, to be with us "always, to the very end of the age"[7]

The reality of Christ's real presence is essential to the achievement of his mission. Nothing less is required to transform sinful creatures into the restored image of God. In fact, nothing less can cause us to show the least resemblance to our Savior. In other

---

[6] Stevick. *Altar's Fire*, 93.
[7] Matthew 28:20, NIV..

words, real presence is absolutely necessary to God's design and our destiny.

This is also why merely remembering Jesus as a long ago hero, whom we admire and whose teachings we still value, will always fall short of his ongoing role in our lives and in the Church. Such remembering cannot sufficiently motivate our discipleship, overcome the obstacles we face, bind us together as vine and branches, or nourish us on the road to glory. "Jesus, through the Spirit and the sacrament, effects a transformation in believers."[8]

The Wesley hymns that focus on the incarnation do not merely extol an historic event, or take us on a sentimental journey. Instead they help us to access the grace and spiritual influence of God's ultimate incursion into our world. The Wesley hymns on the Lord's Supper carry us deeper than recollection or even gratitude could accomplish; deep into the heart and mind of God, beyond detours and distractions, into what early Methodists often called "heaven below."[9]

These Eucharistic hymns convey the whole panorama of the grace the Sacrament contains:

> ... Take, eat, this is my body given,
> To purchase life and peace for you;
> Pardon, and holiness, and heaven.... (HLS 1.)

The "great salvation" sought after in hymn #15 includes every manifestation of grace, from Christ' initial pursuit to final victory in the realms of glory:

> ... Show us all thy great salvation,
> God of truth, and God of love. ...
>
> Give us worthily to adore Thee;
> Thou our full redeemer be;
> Give us pardon, grace, and glory,

---

[8] Stevick. *Altar's Fire*, 105.
[9] Lester Ruth. *A Little Heaven Below: Worship at Early Methodist Quarterly Meetings*. Nashville, TN: Kingswood, 2000.

Peace, and power, and heaven in Thee.[10]

Most of hymn #20 is devoted to remembering the suffering of Christ, but also the blessings won by that suffering, as we see in these lines, which end the hymn by referring to the ultimate purpose of that suffering:

> ...Till perfected in holiness,
> O remember Calvary,
> And bid us go in peace. (HLS 20.)

The theology of sanctification is well established in the Wesleys' writings as part of the way of salvation. Its ties to Eucharistic theology are also part of the whole panorama of grace, beginning with the Lord's Supper as a "converting ordinance" and extending throughout the entire journey of sanctification.

John Wesley once wrote in his journal, "Ye are witnesses. For many now present know, the very beginning of your conversion to God. (perhaps, in some, the first deep conviction) was wrought at the Lord's Supper."[11] We will see that this connection between the Eucharist, repentance, and conversion continued in early North American Methodism. The correspondence among Eucharistic spirituality, evangelism, and transformation toward and within holiness made Holy Communion central, not peripheral or optional, to Methodist worship.

The connection between the Lord's Supper and the Holy Spirit is essential to Wesleyan theology and to the believer's experience of the Sacrament. "The Evangelical Revival brought the sense of the Spirit of God, in life and sacrament, to the foreground. The divine redemptive work is actualized or 'realized,' in the sacramental sign by the Spirit, who is God and who imparts God."

> Come, Holy Ghost, thine Influence shed,
> And realize the sign,
> Thy life infuse into the bread,
> Thy power into the wine. (Stevick. Altar's Fire, 123; HLS 72.)

---

[10] *HLS* 15; the Wesleyan doctrine of holiness was a distinctive emphasis of Methodism, and even more importantly, "the central idea of Christianity." Jesse T. Peck. *The Central Idea of Christianity*. Boston, MA: Henry V. Degen, 1856.

[11] Rattenbury. *Eucharistic Hymns*, 7.

Ernest Rattenbury and Lorna Khoo furnish impressive examples of the demand for, and participation in, Church of England Communion, against the background of typical Anglican neglect in that day, giving us a clear and compelling picture of Wesley's evangelical sacramentalism.

> The general neglect of Eucharistic worship in the eighteenth century in the Church of England is noted by all Anglican authorities. Archbishop Secker, when Bishop of Oxford, in a charge to his clergy actually found it necessary to recommend that there should be at least one celebration in the long interval between Whitsuntide [the season of Pentecost] and Christmas. In many churches there were only three celebrations in the year. Generally speaking, the Sacrament seems to have been little observed.

Rattenbury sees "a marked improvement" in this situation "as a result of Wesley's preaching."[12]

He continues:

> This enthusiasm for Holy Communion was the result of zeal kindled in the hearts of the people by the flaming message of the love of God which they received from the Methodist preachers....
>
> There can be no doubt that Holy Communion was the central devotion of the Evangelical Revival. It was not only the special devotion of the Wesleys, whose early training would largely account for that, but quite a conspicuous feature of the devotional life of the early Methodist preachers. Over and over again they refer to blessings received at the Lord's Table. Fervid evangelists as they were, they knew where to seek the power of their evangelism.
>
> (Rattenbury. Eucharistic Hymns, 3-4.)

John Wesley took notice in his journal of some dramatic responses of early British Methodists to his emphasis on the Sacrament. He mentions one occasion "when we had about 800 communicants," and another where Wesley and one of his assistants administered Communion to a like number. Once in London, "The number of communicants was so great that I was obliged to

---

[12] Rattenbury. *Eucharistic Hymns*, 2.

consecrate thrice"; "I preached and with Dr. Coke's assistance administered the Sacrament to 11 or 12,00 [sic] communicants."[13]

The Wesleys, in their ceaseless efforts to shape and steer their movement, its leaders and members, emphasized constant Communion, which emphasis remained itself a constant, even amid the swirling excitement of newer forms of worship and evangelism. In the coming heyday of the camp meeting, it may have seemed that such "extraordinary means of grace" had eclipsed sacramental means, but in fact the Lord's Supper remained a fixed component of those gatherings, providing a spiritual model for their ongoing impact at their culmination. The placement of the sacrament at or near the end of quarterly and camp meetings gathered up he experiences and fellowship of the entire event in preparation for a memorable, powerful send off.

> What was it that the early Methodists found in the sacrament that led them to crowd the communion tables by the hundreds and thousands? What was it that the Wesleys believed about the sacrament which set it apart from other 'means of grace?' If eucharistic spirituality is a hallmark of Wesleyan spirituality, what does Wesleyan eucharistic spirituality look like? What is the future of this spirituality in Methodism? (Lorna Lock-Nah Khoo. Wesleyan Eucharistic Spirituality: Its Nature, Sources and Future. Adelaide, Australia, 2005, xvi.) Khoo cites further examples from Wesley in England and Ireland, 1-3.)

Heading off in droves for Communion made for a dramatic symbol of the spiritual impact of Wesley's revivals. It represented the people's determination that the impact should be a lasting one, and it expressed a connection between wildfire and tradition, novelty and excitement on the one hand; permanence and steadfastness on the other. The similarity of Wesley's prayer book to the original indicates what little change Wesley thought was needed in the traditional liturgy.

The Wesleys' devotion to Eucharistic worship was shared by George Whitefield [1714-70], who had taken part in some of Scotland's great Eucharistic festivals and had established his own rep-

---

[13] Rattenbury. *Eucharistic Hymns*, 3.

utation as an evangelist in America. The Scottish festivals could be enormous, with spiritual dynamics that made them precursors of North America's camp meetings.[14]

One great need of revivals and revivalists was a powerful inspiration for their ministry; a deep spiritual well to nourish and guide everything they believed and did. "The great Evangelical Revivalists knew that Evangelism could only be grounded on worship, and that the central act in Christian worship is at the table of the Lord, in keeping the command: "Do this in remembrance of me."

There is a crucial distinction in John Wesley's thinking between the Roman Catholic doctrine of transubstantiation, which he strongly denies, and the more widely held teaching and experience of Eucharistic presence, which he strongly affirms. In other words, he saw no necessary connection between real presence and transubstantiation, and no weakening of real presence by their separation. In his sermon on "The Means of Grace," he says,

> Is not the eating of the bread and the drinking of that cup, the outward and visible means whereby God conveys unto our souls all that spiritual grace, and joy in the Holy Ghost which were purchased by the body of Christ once broken, and the blood of Christ once shed for us? Let all, therefore, who truly desire the grace of God, eat of that bread, and drink of that cup." (Rattenbury. Eucharistic Hymns, 7.)

What the Church and the revival needed was the reliable, transformative power of grace. Wesley referred with approval to the patristic understanding of the Eucharist as "the *grand channel* whereby the grace of the Spirit was conveyed to all the souls of the children of God" For instance, for Wesley, Communion functioned as sign and means of forgiveness. For this reason, "Wesley believed that the Lord's Supper was actually a converting ordinance."[15] "There are means of grace, that is outward ordi-

---

[14] Arthur Fawcett. *The Cambuslang Revival (etc.)*. Edinburgh, UK & Carlisle, PA: Banner of Truth, 1971, 114-122; Leigh Eric Schmidt. *Holy Fairs: Scottish Communions and American Revivals in the Early Modern Period*. Princeton, NJ: Princeton University Press, 1989, 3-4, 15-17, 19-20.

[15] Rattenbury. *Eucharistic Hymns*, 7.

nances, whereby the inward grace of God is ordinarily conveyed to man; whereby the faith that brings salvation is conveyed to them who before had it not. ...one of these is the Lord's supper." In fact, Communion was God's way for us to experience and proclaim grace at every stage of life and faith. Wesley put theological guard rails around his strong affirmation of real presence by denying anything automatic or intrinsic about the way Sacraments "worked." He said that "Their benefits depended on the faith of those who used the means, as well as upon the means they used."[16] yet the needed faith could result from Eucharistiic grace. Scholars of these hymns arrive at a fair and accurate picture of the Wesleys' theology of the Eucharist through a careful reading of their hymns alongside a seventeenth-century Anglican theologian who strongly influenced their ideas, and who shared with them a similar perspective.[17] Since the hymns represent their considered conclusions, hammered out over time and renewed in the context of worship, it seems best to call upon them, rather than Daniel Brevint, as our chief resource for understanding Wesleyan Eucharistic theology. "The Hymn-book contained the avowed doctrine of the Wesleys, continually preached to and sung by the Methodist people in the eighteenth century and even after." Rattenbury. *Eucharistic Hymns*, 8.)

The Wesleys' Catholic sounding approach to the Eucharist has a more ancient source than the western middle ages and subsequent controversies.

> The Catholicism of the Wesleys ... was never medieval, but always ante-Nicene. They honored and so far as possible observed and restored the customs of the Christianity of the first three centuries. John regarded the works of the Apostolic Fathers as first-rate authorities only subordinate to the New Testament itself.[18] (Khoo. Wesleyan Eucharistic Spirituality, 115-123.)

---

[16] John Emory, ed. *The Journal of the Reverend John Wesley, A.M.* New-York, NY: J. Emory & B. Waugh, 1832, Nov. 10, 1739, I:167; Rattenbury. *Eucharistic Hymns*, 8.

[17] Daniel Brevint. *The Christian Sacrament and Sacrifice: by way of Discourse, Meditation, and Prayer, upon the Nature, Parts, and Blessings of the Holy Communion (etc.)*. Farmington Hills, MI: Gale, 2018.

[18] Khoo. Wesleyan Eucharistic Spirituality, 115-123.

From this vantage point, they could identify with Brevint's "anti-Puritan," but "also anti-Roman" stance on key Sacramental issues. Brevint could write on "The Depth and Mystery of the Roman Mass," while rejecting transubstantiation and repeated priestly sacrifice.[19] There seems to be an assumption out there that faith in the physical transformation of bread and wine is necessarily the highest and most complete affirmation of real presence. The Catholic doctrine was put forth authoritatively in this statement from the Council of Trent:

> ... after the consecration of bread and wine, our Lord Jesus Christ, true God and man, is truly, really and substantially contained under the appearance of those sensible elements.
>
> ...
>
> Immediately after the consecration, the true body of the Lord – and his true blood – exist under the appearance of bread and wine, together with his soul and divinity. (quoted in Nathan Mitchell. Real Presence: The Work of Eucharist. Notre Dame, IN: Notre Dame Center for Pastoral Liturgy, 2011, 3.)

John Strynkowsi explains some of the development of the doctrine and the fact that, while very old, the language and philosophical analysis embodied in transubstantiation are far from ancient:

> In the late eleventh century theologians described the change that takes place at the Eucharist in terms of a change in the substance of bread and wine, which undergoes transformation into the substance of the Lord's body and blood. The term transubstantiation itself is found only in the twelfth century and was subsequently used at Lateran IV (1215).
>
> ...
>
> In response to opposition to transubstantiation from the Reformers of the sixteenth century, the Council of Trent in 1551 affirmed that the substance of bread and wine is changed into that of Christ's body and blood.

---

[19] Rattenbury. *Eucharistic Hymns*, 11.

...

> Trent's use of the word [transubstantiation] was intended not to explain how the change takes place but to provide a term that describes what takes place. Theological attempts in the latter part of the twelfth century to define the substance (transignification and transfinalization) led Pope Paul VI to insist in Mysterium Fidei that the new meaning and finality of the consecrated bread and wine are grounded in the new ontological reality of the presence of the body and blood of the Lord.[20]

Instead, Wesleyan theology sees the transformation as spiritual and purposeful. Transubstantiation focuses on a change in the elements; Wesleyan Eucharistic theology focuses on a change in their meaning and in the divine reality they convey – their power to signify and focus the delivery of transforming grace. This transformation is in no way of a lesser order. In fact, it keeps our attention on Jesus' original intent for the supper and steers us away from what can become a largely materialistic preoccupation. The Wesleyan view does not compromise or dilute the truth of Jesus' words of institution. Meanwhile, we can respect the care taken in the doctrine of transubstantiation to guard the Church's awareness of the real presence and to support the deep reverence for that presence that typifies Catholic spirituality. Rattenbury writes regarding the careful balance required in order to understand Wesley's thought in context,

> The Wesley doctrine, while anti-Zwinglian is undoubtedly anti-Roman. Often the accusation of Romanism arises from people who hold a mere memorialist theory of the Eucharist, which Wesley would have considered as defective in sacramental doctrine as he would have considered the Roman excessive. (Rattenbury. 13.)

> The Wesleys did not only remember Calvary, but expected to meet the Lord at His Table. They knew that Christ was alive, and believed that He was really present and working, in the Eucharist. This working was in a specific manner in the hearts of people

---

[20] John J. Strynkowski. "Transubstantiation" in Richard P. McBrien, ed. The Harper Collins Encyclopedia of Catholicism. New York, NY: Harper Collins, 1995, 1264.

through the instrumentality of the divinely appointed ordinance which was a means of present graces. (Rattenbury. 3; 27.)

Daniel Brevint articulated the point in a way that appealed greatly to the Wesleys and demonstrates the heart of their view of Christ's presence in the Eucharist:

> The sacrament ordained by Christ the night before he suffered, which St. Paul calls The Lord's Supper, is without doubt, one of the greatest mysteries of godliness, and the most solemn feast of the Christian religion. At the holy table the people meet to worship, and God is present to meet and bless his people. Here we are in a special manner invited to offer up to God our souls, our bodies, and whatever we can give: and God offers to us the body and blood of his Son, and all the other blessings which we have need to receive. So that the holy Sacrament, like the ancient passover, is a great mystery, consisting of Sacrament and Sacrifice, that is, of the religious service which the people owe to God, and of the full salvation which God has promised to his people.
>
> ...
>
> The Lord's Supper was chiefly ordained for a Sacrament, 1. To represent the sufferings of Christ which are past, whereof it is a memorial 2. To convey the first fruits of these sufferings, in present graces, whereof it is a means and 3. To assure us of glory to come, whereof it is an infallible pledge.
>
> ...
>
> This Sacrament ... makes the thing which is represented as really present for our use, as if it were new done. (John Wesley. The Christian Sacrament and Sacrifice: Extracted from a late Author (Daniel Brevint). London. UK: G. Paramore, A2; 4A.)

The Wesleys succeeded in promoting frequent reception of the sacrament. What accounted for their success?

Firstly, it could be due to their high view of holy communion and their example which underlined their teaching. These would be known to all their people through their published writings. John and Charles Wesley grew up in an environment where the eucharist was highly respected and frequently celebrated.

This environment included the influence of their family and schooling. Diocesan records, based on clergy responses to questions from the bishop, indicate that Samuel Wesley, John and Charles' father, was accustomed to offering Communion far more frequently than was generally the case. In the years 1705 – 1723, Samuel served the Eucharist monthly at Epworth, compared to a typical pattern of three times a year for clergy generally. (Khoo. 4; R. E. G. Cole, ed. *Speculum Dioceseseos Lincolniensis,* sub episcopis Gul: Wake et Edm: Gibson, A.D. 1705–1723, Pt. 1, p..xii. Church of England, Lincoln. Saltergate, Lincoln, UK, Issued for the Lincoln Record Society by W.K. Morton & Sons, 1913. https://hdl.handle.net/2027/mdp.39015033837264.)

> Throughout his life, John Wesley communicated very frequently. ... in 1740, he communicated forty out of fifty-two Sundays, had fifty-eight weekday celebrations in a space of one year. In the last nine years of his life ... When weekday communions are added to regular Sunday ones, he would have communicated some fifteen times in one month, an average of once every other day. ... throughout his lifetime, John received on an average of once every four to five days."[21]

Early Methodism in its formative years in Britain and Ireland practiced and taught a Eucharistic theology and spirituality that was thoroughly integrated with its characteristic emphases on conversion and sanctification. We now need to explore the efforts of John Wesley and other leaders to maintain this theology and practice among Methodists in North America and how the original vision fared as Methodism crossed a continent.

---

[21] Khoo. 7, following John C. Bowmer. The Sacrament of the Lord's Supper in Early Methodism. London: Dacre, 1951.

Chapter 3

John Wesley's Hope and Provision for American Methodist Worship

I also advise the elders to administer the supper of the Lord on every Lord's day.[1]

John Wesley viewed worship as central to Methodism's mission as it extended its reach in the New World. While this was clearly an evangelistic mission, there was a distinctive content to its message and its way of life. Sanctifying grace and the pursuit of Christian perfection – "Scriptural holiness" – would be sought and offered across the North American continent and beyond in every way possible, but chiefly in the context of worship, which of course included the Eucharist.

Wesley did not leave that worship to chance. As North American Methodists moved toward autonomy (1784) and propelled their movement westward across British North America and the recently independent United States, he sent a revision of the Anglican prayer book to give structure and content to their worship. Wesley treasured *The Book of Common Prayer* and wanted his movement to continue to enjoy and share its blessings. To that end he devoted considerable time and thought to produce a sizable tome. The edition I have is more than 500 pages long, and while much

---

[1] John Wesley.

of its content is carried over from the standard 1662 prayer book, some was edited to conform to practical requirements and preferences of new and growing lands. Today Wesley's efforts seem out of step with the rough and tumble frontiers they were designed to serve, and even the more settled communities along the coasts. Yet there are portions of the services for Baptism, the Lord's Supper, marriage, and ordination, for example, that have remained in use in various Wesleyan denominations to, or nearly to, this day. While Wesley's prayer book did not live up to its editor's hopes and expectations, it did provide forms for many important occasions, as well as theological grounding in a turbulent world and in sometimes meandering and conflicted churches.

Wesley's vision for Methodist worship in North America is clear from his cover letter to Bishops Thomas Coke [1747-1814] and Francis Asbury [1745-1816] "and our Brethren in NORTH-AMERICA:"

> By a very uncommon train of providences, many of the provinces of North America are totally disjoined from their mother country, and erected into independent states. The English government has no authority over them, either civil or ecclesiastical, any more than over the States of Holland. A civil authority is exercised over them, partly by the Congress, partly by the provincial Assemblies. But no one either exercises or claims any ecclesiastical authority at all. In this peculiar situation some thousands of the inhabitants of these States desire my advice, and in compliance with their desire, I have drawn up a little sketch.
>
> Lord King's account of the primitive church convinced me many years ago, that Bishops and Presbyters are the same order, and consequently have the same right to ordain. For many years I have been importuned from time to time, to exercise this right, by ordaining part of our travelling preachers. But I have still refused, not only for peace' sake, but because I was determined, as little as possible to violate the established order of the national church to which I belonged.
>
> But the case is widely different between England and North-America. Here there are Bishops who have a legal jurisdiction. In America there are none, neither any parish ministers. So that for

some hundred miles together there is none either to baptize or to administer the Lord's supper. Here therefore my scruples are at an end: and I conceive myself at full liberty, as I violate no order and invade no man's right, by appointing and sending labourers into the harvest.

I have accordingly appointed Dr. COKE and Mr. FRANCIS ASBURY, to be joint superintendents over our brethren in North-America: As also RICHARD WHATCOAT [1736-1806] and THOMAS VASEY [1745-1826], to act as Elders among them, by baptizing and administering the Lord's supper. And I have prepared a liturgy little differing from the church of England (I think, the best constituted national church in the world) which I advise all the travelling preachers to use, on the Lord's day, in all their congregations, reading the litany only on Wednesdays and Fridays, and praying extempore on all other days. I also advise the elders to administer the supper of the Lord on every Lord's day.

If any one will point out a more rational and scriptural way, of feeding and guiding those poor sheep in the wilderness, I will gladly embrace it. At present I cannot see any better method than I have taken.[2]

The most important connection for our purposes is that between Wesley's sermon on "The Duty of Constant Communion" and his advice to "the elders to administer the supper of the Lord on every Lord's day." We will take a look at the extent to which Methodists followed Wesley's advice in "feeding and guiding those poor sheep in the wilderness," and how they adapted his advice to their new and ever changing situation. One circumstance that would change was the distance from their countries of origin and from Wesley himself. They kept in touch with their home base by regular correspondence, as they had in Britain and Ireland, but they were writing to each other from different worlds. The time required for letters and responses to cross the ocean and the near impossibility of face to face supervision and consultation meant that most direct communication would have to be

---

[2] Jonathan H. Johnson, ed. John Wesley's Book of Common Prayer (etc.). Marshfield, WI: Furocious, 2018, xv-xvi.

with North American bishops. The separation grew after Wesley's death in 1791, with an even more pronounced shift in the focus of leadership to Asbury and subsequent bishops.

Chapter 4

The Lord's Supper in Early North American Methodism

"The Lord came in power at our sacrament."[1]

The frequency of celebrating Communion would fall far short of Wesley's counsel due to a scarcity of elders. The place and meaning of the Lord's Supper in North America would be lived out in very different circumstances from those at Methodism's origin. The new situations faced by the movement and its leaders would continue and build upon their Wesleyan foundation. The era of American and Canadian pioneers would provide further foundation. In Eucharistic thought and practice, as in so many other facets of their developing cultures, they would establish lasting patterns and cherished experiences that would inspire future generations.

The formative place of early North American roots in the fast growing and quickly changing journey through the 19th century made "the olden time" one of special significance for those who came after. This was recognized by W.P. Strickland, [1809-1884] who wrote or edited many biographies of the early preachers. In the preface to one of those biographies, he wrote,

---
[1] Richard Whatcoat.

Everything relating to the early history of Methodism in this country possesses a value to the members of that denomination, and as the early period of the Church history was the most exciting, the autobiographies of the pioneers will always claim precedence, both in point of importance and interest. [His words are equally true for Methodism North of the border.][2]

In the 1770s, a dispute arose among the American preachers which indicates the importance of the sacraments (and other "ordinances," such as performing marriages and officiating at funerals) to the Methodists of that time. Some of the preachers, who were impatient with rules limiting their ability to administer these rites without the authority conferred by ordination, "seconded the views of the people in respect to having the ordinances among themselves."[3] Francis Asbury and a number of the other preachers held to the existing rule. Asbury wrote:

> For many years I have been importuned from time to time to exercise this right [of presbyters to ordain, an interpretation of the practice of the "primitive Church" held by some Anglicans and eventually acted upon by Wesley] by ordaining part of our travelling preachers, but I have still refused, not only for peace' sake, but because I was determined as little as possible to violate the established order of the established order of the national Church to which I belong. Asbury's words repeat John Wesley's reticence in exercising leadership that would challenge long established precedents.[4]

The pressure to provide sacraments, and the inadequacy of an earlier reliance on Episcopal clergy, borrowed from the English Wesleyans, made it clear that their situation would not long be tenable.

The people began to ask for the ordinances, and as they could

---

[2] W.P. Strickland, ed. Autobiography of Dan Young [1783-1867], A New England Preacher of the Olden Time. New York: Carlton & Porter, 1860, 3-4.

[3] Nathan Bangs. *The Life of the Rev. Freeborn Garrettson (etc.)*, New-York: Emory & Waugh, 1829, 110; 119-122.

[4] W.P. Strickland. The Pioneer Bishop: The Life and Times of Francis Asbury. Manchester, UK: David Kelly & London, UK; Simpkin, Marshall & Company, 1860, 64.

see no reason why those who ministered to them the word of life should not also administer the sacraments of baptism and the Lord's supper, they became more and more earnest in their demands. That their ministers, as well as themselves, should be obliged to go to the Episcopal clergy and receive the sacrament at their hands, was something they could not ... understand. Nor were the people alone in these views and feelings. The preachers at the south pressed the matter upon the attention of the Conference, and there were strong indications of a separation unless the demand was met, (Strickland. Asbury, 46,)

Lester Ruth offers further context for this demand:

Like many other eighteenth- and early- nineteenth-century evangelicals, Methodists evidenced a real desire for the Lord's Supper. In 1806 Francis Ward speaks of how New York Methodists encountered Christ as the sacrament was administered in a camp meeting.

The Lord spread a table for his people in the wilderness, and hundreds partook of the sacramental bread and wine, the symbols of the Redeemer's passion. There they commemorated his dreadful sufferings, and covenanted with him anew, and there they received fresh effusions of his love.[5]

"A table in the wilderness," where people's lives were transformed by "fresh effusions" of Christ's love, is an excellent picture of his real, sacramental presence among these early Methodists. No wonder they "evidenced a real desire for the Lord's Supper."

Asbury's resistance was superseded by Wesley's action in providing an ordained ministry for the Methodists in America. Until that change came, Freeborn Garrettson [1752-1827] worked to keep the connection together. The Christmas Conference and its establishment of the Methodist Episcopal Church constituted a major breakthrough by providing the necessary ordained clergy from within its own ranks. The really interesting point in this struggle is the passionate desire of laity to have access to the Lord's Supper and the other "ordinances."

---

[5] Lester Ruth. Early Methodist Life and Spirituality. Nashville, TN: Kingswood, 2005, 214..

Devereux Jarratt [1733-1801], an Anglican evangelical who was sympathetic to the Methodists, from time to time invited them to receive Communion in his church, baptized Methodists, and even invited Garrettson to preach in his church. Garrettson and Methodists generally would remember his hospitality with gratitude. Garrettson said, "I have had ... some happy seasons in his congregation, particularly on sacramental occasions. At one time about three hundred of his parishioners communed, and the place seemed awful on account of the power and presence of God."[6] That "awful" sense of "the power and presence of God" would return often among the Methodists, especially during camp and quarterly meetings, including at the Lord's Supper. Jesse Lee [1758-1816] wrote that Jarratt...

> ...was disposed to assist the Methodists, both by his advice and by his zealous labours, at all times when convenient. His piety and humility, were such as to endear him to all the sincere followers of Christ. The power of the God of Elijah generally attended his ministry; and at that time the Methodists, having no ordained ministers, found the services of Mr. J. peculiarly acceptable, as from him they could receive the ordinances of the Lord's Supper and baptism. Often did the Methodists, in that day, listen with pleasure to the doctrine which fell from his lips, and joyfully assemble around the table of the Lord, to receive from him with great freedom, and with a heart drawn out in love to the souls of the people....[7]

Lee said that those times of worship led by Jarratt inspired him for his own ministry. (Thrift. *Lee*, 66.)

A provision of an early worship book (1786) disqualified slave owners from receiving Communion; "No person holding slaves shall, in future, be admitted into society, or to the Lord's Supper, till he previously complies [with our policies on slavery]. This rule lost some of its force, however, when it was followed by another one, which said, "These rules are to affect the members of our society no farther than as they are consistent with the laws of the

---

[6] Bangs. Garrettson, 130.

[7] Minton Thrift, ed. Memoirs of the Rev. Jesse Lee. New-York, NY: N. Bangs & T. Mason, 1823, 65-66.

states in which they reside." Even so the earlier provision for excommunication shows how seriously Methodism took both slavery and Communion.[8] Another indication of the serious nature of this holy meal is a reference in Asbury's *Journal* to fasting in connection with the sacrament.[9]

One of Garrettson's early appointments took him to Nova Scotia, where he served for a time with Willian Black, the pioneer superintendent of Methodism in the Maritimes. On one occasion, amid successful preaching engagements, Garrettson mentions "administering baptism to nineteen, and the Lord's Supper to about forty, most of whom he trusted loved God and one another."[10] Even though his remarks about the event are brief, the connection between Communion and community is clearly present, and the proximity to the celebration of Baptism for nineteen suggests a strong connection with an effective evangelistic mission.

Garrettson's biography notes observances of the Lord's Supper later in his career, including one in 1827, in New York City. After preaching on II Peter 3:18, he

> ...then administered the sacrament of the Lord's Supper to a large number of communicants. It was remarked by some who were present on that occasion, that Mr. Garrettson preached with unusual warmth and energy, a Divine unction attending the word. Thus this venerable servant of God closed his public labours in pressing upon his brethren the necessity of going forward in the "work of faith and labour of love," and in participating with him in "drinking of the fruit of the vine" in anticipation of drinking it anew with them in the kingdom of God. (Bangs. Garrettson, 316.)

This celebration now seems especially poignant in that it came not long before Garrettson's death. In conversations with his friend and colleague Nathan Bangs, he testified, "I am filled with the perfect love of God." He also made it plain that his testimony rested entirely on grace: "My hope is all founded in the

---

[8] Strickland. *Asbury*, 83; Cf. 120.
[9] *Journal of Rev. Francis Asbury*, New-York: Lane & Scott, 1852, 1: 140.
[10] Bangs. *Garrettson*, 157.

infinite merits of the Lord Jesus; in this hope I enjoy unspeakable consolation."[11]

How appropriate that his sermon on growing in grace, his reflection on the Lord's Supper, and his witness on Christian perfection, should occupy those moments at the end of his extraordinary life and ministry, as he was about to make his transition into the fullness of God's kingdom.

Richard Whatcoat, who like Garrettson took part in the 1784 Christmas Conference, would later become one of the bishops of the Methodist Episcopal Church. Nearly two months prior to that gathering, Whatcoat and Thomas Coke were traveling through Delaware when they stopped near Dover to lead a sizable congregation in worship. "Dr. Coke preached, and we gave the sacrament to some hundreds. We held a love-feast, and a more comfortable time I have not enjoyed in years."[12]

Not long after that, Coke, Whatcoat, and Francis Asbury met near Baltimore to plan for the upcoming conference. The conference itself set basic parameters for the new church, including these concerning worship:

> We agreed to form a Methodist Episcopal Church, in which the Liturgy, as presented by The Rev. John Wesley, should be read, Sacraments to be administered by a Superintendent. Elders, and Deacons, who shall be ordained by a Presbytery, using the Episcopal form, (as prescribed in the Rev. Mr. Wesley's prayer book). (Phoebus. Whatcoat, 21; Jonathan H. Johnson, ed. John Wesley's The Book of Common Prayer.[13]

Following the conference, Whatcoat pursued an arduous schedule: "preaching almost every day, and sometimes twice a day, with the administering of the ordinances of Baptism and the Lord's Supper, kept me in full employ...." Among his many stops, he mentions one called Kent Island, where "we had a precious time at a quarterly meeting ... especially at the Sacrament." At an-

---

[11] Bangs. *Garrettson*, 317.

[12] William Phoebus. *Memoirs of the Rev. Richard Whatcoat (etc.)*. New-York, Joseph Allen, 1828, 19-20.

[13] The Sunday Service of the Methodists in North America, 1789). Marshfield, WI: Furocious, 2018.

other quarterly meeting, he says, "the Lord came in power at our Sacrament; the cries of the mourners, and the ecstasies of believers were such that the preacher's voice could scarcely be heard, for the space of three hours; many were added to the number of true believers. (Phoebus. *Whatcoat.* 23-24.) This kind of report fills the pages of Whatcoat's memoirs of quarterly meetings and resembles closely the experience of participants at the camp meetings that swept across the continent, in and beyond the nineteenth century. Such experiences of the presence and power of God were certainly not limited to the Lord's Supper, but they could often enough be found there. Whatcoat was well prepared, along with Asbury and other bishops, to champion the camp meetings as major forms of worship, spirituality, and evangelism for their movement.

Many of the biographies, autobiographies, and early histories of Methodism contain references ranging from brief mentions to extended reflections of early preachers on the celebration of Holy Communion as they experienced and observed it. Sometimes there was a short indication at least of the mood of the event or the response of the participants. In one of these, Christian Newcomer [1749-1830] recorded his disappointment: "The ordinance of the Lord's Supper was administered, but no excitement was produced." Others mentioned a Communion only briefly, perhaps indicating a Scriptural context, such as this one from Henry Boehm [1775-1875]: "After the sermon, the Lord's Supper was administered, and Jesus was made known to us in the breaking of bread." Yet even this short reference affirms the Lord's presence in the sacred meal. By way of contrast, Newcomer also recorded this example: "We administered the Lord's supper, and the converting power of God was signally displayed; many came voluntarily forward and entreated us to pray for them; several obtained pardon of sin in the blood of the Lamb." In another, we read of a prolonged effect when, "many hundreds came to the Lord's table, singing and praying with the mourners, during the whole night. A great many were happily converted, and found peace for their souls in the blood of the Lamb." Here we see a familiar scene from many quarterly and camp meetings, where the already converted form a community of prayer around spiritual newcomers, welcoming them into the kingdom. No wonder Bishop Newcomer could say of another such gathering, "it proved a happy day to many souls."[14]

There was power in these Eucharistic feasts both to transform and unite participants, even across unlikely and formidable barriers. Bishop Newcomer tells of one such Communion:

> The sacrament of the Lord's Supper was administered; more than 500 white persons and 29 Indians came forward to the Lord's table. Before the meeting was brought to a close, the grace of God was poured out in such plentiful showers, that I do not recollect ever to have witnessed any thing to equal it: unto the Most High be all the glory. (Newcomer. 262.)

Another Evangelical preacher and bishop, John Seybert [1791-1860], reported a camp meeting Communion where the power of God's presence was evident: "At a camp meeting near Orwigsburg, Pennsylvania, in 1835, in the preparation service of the Lord's supper, some sank as though dead, into the deep sea of God's love."[15] O'Malley points out that, for the Evangelical Association branch of the Methodist tradition: "The Lord's Supper was not a service of memorial to Christ in a cognitive sense alone. ... The Supper visibly signified an inward, continuous communion with Christ." Thus its power to transform. (O'Malley. 161.)

Newcomer's reference to the Lord's table as a meeting place and source of unity for people of various ethnicities was far from unique. Canadian Methodist historian George Playter described a quarterly meeting among indigenous people, led by a white presiding elder and an Ojibwe Methodist preacher, held at Rice Lake in Upper Canada (Ontario), showing its emotional impact on participants:

> The quarterly meeting in May was attended by Elder [William]

---

[14] Christian Newcomer. *The Life and Journal of the Rev'd Christian Newcomer (etc.).* Hagers-Town, MD: F.G.W. Kapp, 1834, 75; 282; 136; 69; Joseph B. Wakeley, ed. *Reminiscences, Historical and Biographical ... by Rev, Henry Boehm.* New York: Carlton & Porter, 1866, 93.

[15] John Steven O'Malley. *John Seybert and the Evangelical Heritage.* Lexington, KY: Emeth, 2008, 105.

Case [1780-1855] and Peter Jones [1802-1856]. ... the services were seasons of refreshing, and the power of the Lord rested upon the people. Eighty-five natives partook of the Lord's Supper, mostly all weeping aloud, and some were so overcome that they could not rise from their knees, and were carried off by their friends.

Playter also recorded this instance of the Lord's Supper being celebrated by Indians and whites together at an 1826 camp meeting on the Bay of Quinte near Adolphustown, Upper Canada:

> On Saturday and Sunday, the congregation increased to between three and four thousand people. Beaver [an exhorter] spoke to his people with great fluency. ... At the close of the meeting, every Indian was converted, and happy in the Saviour's love. On Monday, the Lord's Supper was given to the Indians and the whites. ... The camp meeting resulted in the conversion of ninety persons, and gave a new impulse to the religious societies around. As yet, these Indians knew but one hymn, "O, for a thousand tongues to sing my great Redeemer's praise," and one tune. This hymn they sang, over and over, as if always new and always good.[16]

At Green Bay, "on the western side of Lake Michigan," circuit preacher John Clark [1797-1853] and Daniel Adams, "a native preacher in the Mohawk language," served Communion to a diverse group of Indians in 1832. Again we see God bringing people together in peace through this means of grace:

> [After preaching and celebrating baptism, Clark] then gave the Lord's Supper to thirty-five or forty Indians, all "meekly kneeling upon their knees." Among these were some Presbyterians as well as Methodists; and they belonged to three different tribes, Oneidas, Stockbridges [also called the Stockbridge-Munsee band of Mohican Indians], and Tuscaroras. On that occasion the missionary [Clark] says, 'it was truly a season of melting interest [warm, intense, God-centered fellowship]. I have seldom enjoyed one of greater happiness at the table of our blessed Lord.[17] (B.M. Hall. The Life of Rev. John Clark. New York, NY: Carlton & Porter, 1856, 89-90.

---

[16] George F. Playter. The History of Methodism in Canada. Toronto, ON: Anson Green, for the Author, 1862, 357; 280.

[17] B.M. Hall. The Life of Rev. John Clark. New York, NY: Carlton & Porter, 1856, 89-90.

In Canada, Egerton Ryerson [1803-1882], who like William Case devoted considerable effort to ministry among First Nations people, recalled the first service held in a church built specifically for the use of native worshipers. He wrote, "this has been an important day [1826]. We opened the Indian Chapel by holding a love-feast and celebrating the Lord's supper. The Indians with such solemnity and feeling expressed what God had done for them."[18]

In his autobiography, the prominent Ojibwe Methodist preacher Peter Jones (*Keh-ke-wa-guo-na-ba,*) recorded the extensive cooperative ministry that took place involving First Nations and white Methodists, often including the *Lord's Supper.* Here again we find reference to the presence of the Lord in the Eucharistic meal. For example, we have this account from a camp meeting in 1829:

> In the afternoon we met at the chapel for worship. I preached to the Indians on the subject of the Lord's supper. Peter Jacobs [another Ojibwe preacher, c. 1807-1890.] exhorted. We felt the presence of the Lord in our midst ... After the love feast the Lord's supper was given to seventy-one Indians. The Lord poured out his spirit [sic] upon us in a powerful manner, and a number of the women fell to the floor, as if shot down, but rose up again rejoicing in the Lord. My soul was filled with love and gratitude to God. Blessed be His saving power!

Jones gives another account from 1828, where God's powerful grace was at work:

> The Elder [William Case] proceeded to administer the holy communion of the Lord's supper, of which 85 of the natives partook. The power of the Lord rested upon the assembly, and at the close of this service, an overwhelming shower of divine grace descended upon us, and there was a mighty shout in the house. Our Presiding Elder was full of joy, and joined the Indians in their praises of God. Glory be to God for the blessing I received at this meeting!

---

[18] J. George Hodgins, ed. *The Story of My Life, by the Late Rev. Egerton Ryerson (etc.).* Toronto, ON: William Briggs, 1883, 66.

He also recorded an experience at a Yonge Street camp meeting from 1829, again highlighting the way God's power could unify diverse people through an overpowering experience of grace:

> Rev. W[illiam] Ryerson [1797-1872] ... administered the Lord's Supper to many happy souls. The power of the Spirit rested upon both whites and Indians, and several fell to the ground under the power of God, and were obliged to be carried away to their tents. We then formed a procession and marched round the ground, the preachers took the lead, and after going round the ground two or three times they stood in a row and shook hands with the people as they passed by, at the same time singing appropriate hymns. Thus this interesting and profitable meeting closed, and we all went on our journey rejoicing. Before parting with our Schoogog ad Mud Lake brethren I gave them several copies of our Ojebwe Hymn Book, lately printed in New York, which were received with great joy.[19]

Sadly, Julia A.J. Foote [1823-1900], the first woman deacon in the African Methodist Episcopal Zion Church, remembered her parents' experience in a Methodist Episcopal congregation, in which the Lord's Supper was anything but an occasion for unity across cultures.

> They were not treated as Christian believers, but as poor lepers. They were obliged to occupy certain seats in one corner of the gallery, and dared not come down to partake of the Holy Communion until the last white communicant had left the table. ... this was one of the fruits of slavery. Although professing to love the same God, members of the same church, and expecting to find the same heaven at last they could not partake of the Lord's Supper until the lowest of the whites had been served.[20]

In a funeral sermon in memory of African Methodist Episcopal Bishop William Paul Quinn [1788-1873], Benjamin William Arnett [1838-1906] recounted the same pattern Julia Foote de-

---

[19] Peter Jones. Life and Journals of Keh-ke wa-guo-na-ba Rev. Peter Jones). Toronto, ON: Anson Green, Wesleyan Printing Establishment, 1860, 220-221; 143; 225.

[20] Julia A.J. Foote. A Brand Plucked from the Fire. Cleveland, OH: Lauer & Yost, 1881, 11.

scribed, in what had become a standard rendition of a people's painful experience:

> [Following the American Revolution,] while the world was rejoicing at the establishment of a government whose declared principles were universal, political, civil, and religious liberty, and while they were singing the anthems of peace, there was another mighty conflict going on – not on the battle-field, with saber and musket, but in the churches and the social circles of the land. Prejudice, the unrelenting enemy of the oppressed and weak, was asserting its power; and from the year 1787 to 1816, the conflict continued without cessation. The colored portion of the numerous congregations of the North and South were wronged, proscribed, ostracized, and compelled to sit in the back seats in the sanctuary of the Lord. The sons of toil and daughters of oppression remained on these seats for some time hoping that some of the members, at least, would receive a sufficient amount of grace to enable them to treat these children of sorrow with Christian courtesy. But they were doomed to disappointment, for soon bad yielded to worse, and they were sent up in the dusty galleries. There, high above the congregation, they had to serve the Lord silently – for not an amen must come down from among that sable band. These and other indignities our fathers bore with Christian patience for a number of years. They were denied the communion of the Lord's supper until all the white members had partaken. This treatment continued until forbearance ceased to be a virtue, and our fathers drew out from among them; for the watch-fires of soul-freedom were burning in their bosoms. These were kindled and fed by the sentiments of the age in which the lived; for on every side could be heard the watch-word of the nation – "All men are born free and equal, and endowed by their Creator with certain inalienable rights, among which are life, liberty, and the pursuit of happiness."
>
> The first meeting was held in the blacksmith shop of [later Bishop] Richard Allen, [1760-1831], in Philadelphia, Pennsylvania...[21]

---

[21] Benjamin William Arnett. Sermon in Memoriam: Funeral Services in Respect to the Memory of Rev. William Paul Quinn. Richmond, IN: Warren Chapel, 1873, 12-13.

Thankfully, there are more encouraging reports, including a very early journal entry from Francis Asbury, illustrating a foundational attitude necessary to produce active Christian compassion and justice. In 1772, Asbury wrote about administering the Lord's Supper in John Street Church.] "At the table I was greatly affected with the sight of the negroes, seeing their sable faces at the table of the Lord."[22]

Being "greatly affected" with positive emotions generated during Holy Communion was often included in descriptions of those services. Jesse Lee once described the impact he felt in a Communion service that took place following ordination at an annual conference where Bishop Asbury presided : "Then the Lord's Supper was administered, and we had a very solemn time. I found my soul much quickened and refreshed." Of another occasion, a quarterly meeting, he wrote, "we administered the Lord's Supper, and many of the communicants were bathed in tears." In yet another Lord's Supper, Lee tells us, "At still another gathering,

> "Then we had the Lord's Supper, and a great many communicants, together with twelve preachers; the people were greatly affected at the table, and many of the spectators who tarried in the house wept freely. I was pleased and surprised to see such a crowd of people at the Lord's table. When I first came among them, about fifteen years ago, they had never seen a Methodist ... but at this time (1808), we have nine local preachers, and, I suppose, about one hundred persons to commune with us. Surely the Lord hath done great things for us.[23]

There are many accounts describing the emotions of communicants, like this one in 1828, from Peter Jones:

> The communion of the Lord's Supper was then administered to about forty-seven [Mohawk and Oneida] Indians, and never did I witness a congregation more solemn and devout than these newly converted Indians; some were so full of the love of God, that with streaming, uplifted eyes, they shouted aloud and praised

---

[22] J.B. Wakeley. *Lost Chapters Recovered from the Early History of American Methodism (etc.)*. New York, NY; Carlton & Porter, 1858, 439-440.

[23] Minton Thrift, ed. Memoir of the Rev. Jesse Lee (etc.). New-York: N. Bangs & T. Mason,1823,, 196; 200; 322.

God for all his mercies. (Peter Jones. Life and Journals, 225.)

Jesse Lee describes a celebration near Lake Champlain, close to the Canadian border: 'our good God was pleased to meet with us at his table, and we did set in heavenly places in Christ Jesus."[24] The testimony that "God was pleased to meet with us at his table" is a familiar way of referring to the presence. The unusual expression ("set in heavenly places") was one of several expressing the heavenly fellowship people experienced at the Lord's Supper.

Given the high impact and deep emotions of these sacred moments, at such an early time, leaders and participants recorded many memorable "firsts" in ministry, including the first Holy Communions celebrated by Methodists. The first camp meeting in Canada, organized by prominent circuit riders Nathan Bangs [1778-1862}, Henry Ryan,[1775-1833] and William Case [1780-1855] was held at Adolphustown, Upper Canada (Ontario) in 1805. Like similar events across the continent, this one included a celebration of the Lord's Supper. Bangs described the camp meeting in considerable detail. Regarding Communion, he wrote, "At noon the Lord's Supper was administered to multitudes, while other multitudes looked on with astonishment and tears." This experience followed a Sunday morning of worship where "the power of the Spirit was manifest throughout the whole encampment, and almost every tent was a scene of prayer." Though he says little about the specifics of the Communion, what he does tells us about what preceded and followed it gives us a picture of continuity spanning much of the day. Prior to the sacrament, "the interest and excitement were so great that while some assembled around the stand [the preachers' platform], a preacher mounted a wagon at a distance and addressed a separate congregation." This was the preparation for all that followed:

> After the sacrament, a young woman, of fashionable and high position in society, was smitten down, and with sobs entreated the prayers of the people. Her sister forced her away. A preacher went forth without the camp and led them both back, followed by quite a procession of their friends. A circle gathered around

---

[24] Thrift, ed. *Lee*, 164; 208; 277.

them and sang and prayed. The unawakened sister was soon upon her knees praying in agony, and was first converted; the other quickly after received the peace of God, and they wept and rejoiced together.[25]

This episode, involving two sisters and their friends, did not occur in isolation but was told as an illustration of what happened on that day at Adolphustown and at thousands of camp meetings across North America. People from all kinds of backgrounds experienced high energy preaching, prayer, and singing, often, but not necessarily among friends. In an outdoor environment, focused upon God and away from distractions, many found forgiveness, peace, purpose, and joy in a new or renewed connection with God and each other in the transforming power of the Spirit. The camp meeting was, and in many places still is, an extraordinary means of grace in which the Lord's Supper, an older, essential means of grace, played/plays a vital role.

James Finley [1781-1856] recalled it as a memorable milestone when he celebrated what he believed was the first Methodist Eucharist in Ohio.

> The writer ... cannot help adverting to the time when he spread the first table for the sacrament of the Lord's supper that was spread north west of the Ohio. When the communicants were called to approach the table, the number did not exceed twenty-five or thirty; this was the sum of all that were in the country. Now the minutes of the annual conferences of Ohio return one hundred thousand regular Church members; so mightily hath the word of God run and prevailed!

Finley also wrote about his own first experience partaking in Communion, at a quarterly meeting in Ohio, led by presiding elder John Sale [1769-1827]. "In the afternoon the sacrament of the Lord's Supper was administered; and as I never had partaken of this holy communion before it was a t1ime of great self-examination, and deliberate, solemn consecration to God on my part. I was much blessed in partaking of the emblems of the broken

---

[25] Abel Stevens. Life and Times of Nathan Bangs, D.D. New York: Carlton & Porter, 1863, 153-154.

body and shed blood of my Redeemer." Methodists often used "Solemn" to describe the seriousness of partakers and the depth of the Impact they felt.[26]

Finley wrote of a lesson he learned at a celebration led by Bishop William Mc Kendree [1757-1835], reflecting a change of heart:

> An incident occurred at this camp meeting of a deeply thrilling character, and one which produced an entire change in my views in regard to the qualifications necessary to partake of the holy communion. I supposed that only such as were converted, and were the children of God by faith in Christ Jesus, were entitled to a place at the Lord's table. There accompanied us to the camp meeting a young lady. To the graces of her person, for she was charmingly beautiful, were added a brilliant mind. She was an amiable and lovely girl, the pride of the neighborhood. Scarcely had we arrived on the ground ere she was convicted. During Saturday and Sunday she seemed to be in the most extreme agony of mind. Her prayers and tears excited the sympathy of all hearts.
>
> On Monday morning the of the Lord's supper was to be administered. After singing ... the ministers were all invited around the table to partake of the holy emblems. The venerable bishop offered the consecratory prayer, and then distributed to the under shepherds the bread and wine. It was a deeply solemn time.
>
> A solemn stillness reigned around, only broken by a deep sigh or a half-suppressed sob, while one after another of that large congregation came to celebrate the scenes of Gethsemane and Calvary. Nearly in front of the bishop, beyond the altar, stood the weeping penitent, reclining her head upon the shoulder of a converted sister, and sobbing as if her heart would break, while she gazed upon the scene. Her appearance and manner attracted the attention of the benevolent M'Kendree, and looking toward her he said, "My child, come here and kneel at the foot of the cross, and you shall find mercy,"
>
> "Do you think," said she, through her tears, "so vile a sinner as I may venture to approach the sacramental board, and take in my

---

[26] W.P. Strickland, ed. *Autobiography of Rev. James B. Finley (etc.)* Cincinnati, OH: Cranston & Curts, 1853, 186.

unholy hands the emblems of the Savior's dying love?"

"Yes, my child; it was just for such sinners as you the blessed Jesus died, and while writhing in his last agony, he demonstrated his willingness and power to save by taking the penitent malefactor with him to heaven."

"Then I'll go to Jesus," said she, and hurrying to the table she fell upon her knees and cried aloud to God. With streaming eyes the bishop administered the bread; and just as her lips tasted the wine of the sacramental cup, pardon was communicated, and heaven sprang up in her heart. Instantly she rose to her feet, and her face shining like that of an angel, while, with an eloquence that went to every heart, she told the simple story of the cross, and the wondrous power of Christ to save. All seemed to partake of the common joy of that renewed spirit.[27]

Along with several details of the way this service was conducted, we see lived out in this episode one of Wesley's major points: we should receive Communion gratefully, out of our genuine need, not out of presumed worthiness. Bishop M'Kendree's pastoral counsel to the young woman in the story was exactly in accord with Wesley's reading of Scripture, with this woman's need, and with the purpose of the camp meeting. Through his example in this situation, the bishop was effectively mentoring at least one young preacher. Finley was learning something important that would serve him well throughout his long and fruitful ministry, including his years as a state prison chaplain. In his prison ministry he lamented public attitudes regarding prisoners and the sacraments:

While talking seriously of the communion of the Lord's supper, the prisoner has often been met with the objection, "But you are in a penitentiary, and public opinion is against you. You cannot participate in the full means of grace and the free blessings of the Gospel, because you have been a sinner." I trust in God that the day is not far distant when the penitentiary will become a place of glorious revivals, and thousands of convicts taste of the riches of grace, and go forth into the world like the demoniac of

---

[27] Strickland, ed. Autobiography of James Finley, 401-402.

the tombs, in their right minds, to tell their families and friends what great things the Lord has done for them. There is nothing to prevent this but the contracted views and prejudices which the managers and directors of prisons have of religion. They are afraid of a noise, or of their popularity – so much that all things must be done just according to their own views and feelings. A cold harangue and long and tedious ceremonies will not awaken a sinner. The Gospel must be preached with the power and demonstration of the Spirit. All else will be but a sounding brass and a tinkling cymbal. Constituents should therefore say to their representatives, "Open the door to the captive, that he may enjoy the benefits of the Gospel of peace – that his chains may fall off, and he be set free by the power of the Holy Spirit. Let him have all the means of grace and the Gospel ordinances when he is prepared to receive them."[28]

The question of qualification to partake in the Lord's Supper met with different responses as Methodists sought to balance the integrity of the sacrament with pastoral openness to the movement of the Spirit. At the beginning, Asbury and Coke put forth the former concern:

We must also observe, that our elders should be very cautious how they admit to the communion persons who are not in our society. It would be highly injurious to our brethren, if we suffered any to partake of the Lord's Supper with them, whom we would not readily admit to our society on application made to us. Those whom we judge unfit to partake of our profitable, prudential means of grace, we should most certainly think improper to be partakers of an ordinance which has been expressly instituted by by Christ himself.[29]

This relatively rigid stance would eventually give way to the more pastoral and evangelistic approach in Finley's story of Bishop Mc Kendree and the young woman. The fluid, intense, and pragmatic environment of a camp meeting called for the kind

---

[28] Benjamin Franklin Tefft, ed. James Bradley Finley, Memorials of Prison Life. Cincinnati: Swormstedt & Poe, 1857, 301-302.

[29] Doctrines and Discipline of the Methodist Episcopal Church, 1798, 119 & 120, quoted in Lester Ruth. Early Methodist Life and Spirituality. Nashville, TN: Kingswood (Abingdon), 2005, 216).

of wisdom and flexibility shown by the bishop and advocated by Finley. The issue here is not carelessness or lack of respect in matters of integrity of the church and its worship. Instead, the issue is the response of the church and its leaders to fast moving situations. Today's open Communion Methodists would be surprised to read the exclusive position of the first bishops, which is more typical of certain bodies of Baptists and Lutherans. The restrictive position does bear resemblance to Wesley's high standards for society and class membership, but not with his characterization of the Lord's Supper as a "converting ordinance." The early Evangelicals also showed an interest in maintaining order by controlling access to the Lord's table. One can see their point in situations where some people's attitudes might be far from solemn and their actions distracting from the purpose at hand, but there had to be room for prevenient and converting grace to bring about an appropriate response.

Peter Jones recalls a challenge from a Church of England minister who accused the Methodists of serving Communion to flagrant sinners and thus bringing disgrace upon their church.

> He ... said that the Methodist preachers had administered the communion to a notorious adulteress.
>
> I was informed by those who were present when the above person alluded to went forward to partake of that ordinance, and they said that she went under disguise, and that the minister did not know her to be of such a character. How careful ought ministers to be in giving the Holy Communion to fit and proper subjects! (Peter Jones. Life and Journals. 275-276.).

We could question whether the understanding of this situation expressed by Peter Jones or the Anglican accuser is the most suitable response, especially without knowing this woman's motivation. But the incident illustrates the church's attempt to guard the integrity of the sacrament while at the same time maintaining its essential purpose as a means of grace. It seems that Jones was much closer to the mark when he approached the sacrament at a quarterly conference in 1825, questioning his own worthiness rather than someone else's: "I do not recollect that ever I felt myself more unworthy of approaching the table of the Lord than I did at this time. O Lord, help me ever to remember the real atonement made for my poor soul." (Jones. *Life and Journal*, 31.)

James Finley recounts an incident late in his life, involving a military officer – a General Long – and his wife, who was part of an Indian nation in northeast Ohio. Finley describes her as "a most worthy, consistent, and zealous member of the Methodist Episcopal Church" who "possessed much of the true Indian character of integrity and perseverance, conjoined with a large share of gentleness and benevolence." He goes on to say: "Her fidelity and devotion as a wife and mother beautifully assorted with the entire consecration of her heart to God. In all the religious exercises she took an active part, and her labors and example were particularly beneficial to her Indian sisters in the Lord."

> This characterization differed markedly from the way Finley describes her husband, yet he also acknowledges the General's redeeming qualities: "Though wicked ... he was not opposed to his wife on account of her religion, but rather assisted than prevented her in the discharge of her religious duties."

In this episode, she decided to attend an "Indian camp meeting." In spite of standing outside the faith, "He had a respect for religious institutions, and would regularly attend, with his wife, at the log church." This camp meeting would do what camp meetings are designed to do, to facilitate Spirit-empowered transformation.

The account begins with the General seated beside his wife at Sunday worship.

> He was an attentive observer of all that transpired, and listened eagerly to all that was said. Those who knew him best, saw from his clouded brow, and his attempts to rally his spirits, that there was something pressing heavily upon his otherwise joyous and happy mind, and they were not much at a loss in conjecturing the cause. The Spirit of God was evidently at work in his heart. His affectionate wife and Indian friends were constant and earnest in pouring out their supplications on his behalf. His convictions increased, notwithstanding all his attempts to shake them off; and when Monday morning came, he was glad to avail himself of

the opportunities his duties afforded in leaving for the muster-field, where companies awaited his inspection. He accordingly mounted his horse and started, but his Christian friends did not give him up. They knew full well that God was at work upon his heart....

What was at stake that caused his friends such concern mixed with hope was the entire trajectory of his life and its fulfillment.

...their anxieties were increased in the conviction that a crisis had arrived in his history which would, in all probability, decide his destiny forever. ... There is a time in the history of every man, when it may be said of him individually, as it was said by the Savior to the scribe, on a certain occasion, "Thou art not far from the kingdom of heaven." When the tide of divine influence is up, and waves of mercy are gathering around, then the soul may start out upon that flood for heaven, but if this influence is resisted, the receding waves will bear away hope and happiness, it may be forever.

The General had not proceeded more than two miles on his journey till his feelings became almost insupportable. He was alone, and there being nothing to divert his mind, he was shut up to himself, and a horror of darkness came upon him. To go farther he felt it would be impossible. The cords of an irresistible influence seemed to be drawing him back, and having reached their utmost tension he must yield or break that influence forever. He turned his horse in the direction of the camp-ground and rode rapidly back. When he arrived the congregation were assembled for the purpose of partaking of the holy communion. The elements of bread and wine had been consecrated by holy hands and prayer, and the pastor was inviting the flock to come forward to the rude altar, and participate in the Eucharistic feast, which every want supplies. He stood and gazed upon the scene. He saw his beloved wife advance and kneel with the whites and Indians that crowded to their places; and as the minister said, "He that confesseth Jesus before men, shall be acknowledged by him in heaven; while he that denieth him shall also be denied at the judgment of the great day," he felt .... that he must forever be separated from his dear wife and the society of all the good, and the scene and associations so affected him that he wept aloud.

This was the beginning of his response to God's prevenient grace, that had been at work through his wife and Christian friends, through the church services he had attended, through the preaching and prayer that were part of this camp meeting, and now through this service of Holy Communion. But the crisis Finley talked about was not yet complete.

> After the sacrament was ended, the presiding elder addressed the congregation touchingly alluding to the scenes of Gethsemane and Calvary, which had been presented to them in the passion and death of the Son of God, and concluded by inviting all who were desirous of fleeing the wrath to come, and of being saved from their sins, to come forward, and kneel at the altar and pray for pardon. Scarcely had he ceased till anxious souls in large numbers pressed to the mercy-seat. The general was standing, in full military costume, at rest, with one hand upon the stake that supported the altar railing. His feelings were wrought up to the highest point of excitement, and unable any longer to restrain his emotion, which was raging with earthquake violence within his soul, he exclaimed, with a loud but tremulous voice, "Quarters! quarters!" my God, quarters! I yield!;" and then fell his whole length upon the ground. He was soon surrounded by the godly, and borne into the altar. The excitement produced by this demonstration, among the whites and Indians, was tremendous; and when they all fell on their knees there went up such a storm of prayer as rent the very heavens. The General wept, and groaned, and prayed for the space of two hours....

This agonizing crisis was repeated often at camp meetings. The Spirit was working a profound transformation in the depths of this man's soul, one that would impact the rest of his life and beyond.

> Hark! A shout, "Glory, glory!" in loud, full bursts, escapes from his lips. "Where am I?" said the converted man. "I never saw so beautiful a place in all my life before." In an instant his wife, who alone had been pouring out her heart to God in her husband's behalf, was at his side, praising God for redeeming grace. They embraced with an affection they never knew before; for they were now one in Jesus. His Indian and white friends turned their prayers into praises....

He was greeted by the warm-hearted chief, Mononcue [prominent Wyandotte chief and Methodist preacher, dates unknown], who embraced him, and said, in broken English, "My brother, you must now fight for King Jesus."[30]

This narrative deserves to be quoted at length for several reasons. It gives us an unusually complete picture of a camp meeting Communion while telling a compelling story of a small group of participants. It takes us into the surprising world of bicultural camp meetings, which were more numerous and more successful than we might have imagined. Finley was appointed to the Wyandotte mission. He was a strong advocate for the indigenous people of northeast Ohio. The story also illustrates the intertwining of revival with the Lord's Supper as they reinforce one another in living out the theology and spirituality of salvation as it was taught by John Wesley. This particular story includes many details left out of other accounts. Here we have the drama taking place at the time of a Eucharistic celebration. No description is given of a formal, written liturgy, so we can't be sure what may have been taken from Wesley's Book of Common Prayer or what may have been extemporaneous. There are clear references to themes in what was said, especially the connection between the Lord's Supper and Christ's sacrifice, re-presented and applied for the camp meeting setting and the situation at hand. There is mention of a presiding elder addressing the congregation, and it is likely that he was the minister who consecrated the elements. Presiding elders often celebrated sacraments at quarterly meetings and were among those in leadership at camp meetings. We hear the minister's invitation to "come forward to the rude altar," indicating the active response of the congregation, who did not remain on their benches, waiting to be served. We also see the community praying fervently for the General and seeing him through his crisis of conviction and repentance to the rejoicing that followed, and the chief (who was also a preacher) giving both welcome and charge the new convert. There is also a fascinating reference to the "eucharistic feast, which every want supplies." Certainly it is possible to claim too much in interpreting this expression, but

---

[30] W.P. Strickland, ed. Sketches of Western Methodism, by James B. Finley. Cincinnati, OH: Methodist Book Concern, Published for the Author, 1855, 526 – 529.

we could err even more seriously by claiming too little.

John Carroll included several mentions of the Lord's Supper in his five-volume work on the early history of Canadian Methodism, *Case and His Contemporaries.* In an early chapter, Carroll quotes quotes Peter Vannest [1759-1850], who substituted for the presiding elder at the Niagara and Long Point Circuits' quarterly meetings in 1803. He mentions regarding Long Point, "At a newly settled place in the Circuit, I appointed a Love feast and Sacrament of the Lord's Supper. It was a new thing there, and many attended." Such was the situation in newly established settlements, that the usual quarterly meeting Communion might be thought of as "a new thing," but greeted with good attendance, probably by people who remembered and understood its meaning from their former communities.[31]

Carroll also relates considerable detail, originally from Nathan Bangs, one of the organizers, about Canada's first camp meeting, held at Adolphustown, Upper Canada (Ontario) in 1805. Included in his account a reference to Holy Communion, recorded elsewhere in the present volume.

In another place, Carroll quotes Henry Boehm's story of an 1811 quarterly meeting in eastern Ontario, in which Bishop Francis Asbury had an important part. A participant recorded of the meeting, "It was a time of power; many of God's people rejoiced, and some mourners found converting grace. On Saturday we had a glorious time in Love-feast, and at the Lord's Supper. Bishop Asbury preached a thrilling sermon from Titus, ii., 11, 12."[32]

Also in quoting Boehm, we have this account of a quarterly meeting, this one at Hay Bay, where the first Methodist church structure was built in 1792. The meticulously restored church is still open for seasonal visitors and occasional worship. The ministers present were among the best known on both sides of the border:

On Friday we rode to Brother John Embury's, Hay Bay. He was

---

[31] John Carroll, *Case and His Contemporaries (etc.).* Toronto: Samuel Rose, 1867, 1: 78-79.
[32] Carroll. *Case,* 1:233.

a nephew of Phillip Embury [1729-75], the Apostle of American Methodism. He was awakened at the age of sixteen under his uncle's preaching in New York. The next day – Saturday – Edward Cooper preached at eleven o'clock, and Henry Ryan and I exhorted.

On the Lord's day we had a glorious love-feast, and at the Lord's Supper He was made known to us in the breaking of bread. In a beautiful grove, under the shade of trees planted by God's own hand, I preached to two thousand people [Carroll: "so many did a Quarterly Meeting draw together in those days."] from Luke xix ;10; John Reynolds [d. 1857] ... and Henry Ryan [1775-1833] exhorted. The sparks flew, and the fire fell. Henry Ryan was from Ireland. He was a powerful man in that day.[33]

Carroll borrows an interesting article from Egerton Ryerson [1803-1882], originally published (1929) in the Christian Guardian, the premier periodical of Methodism in Canada, about a recently deceased minister named Ninian Holmes [1785-1829]. The article refers briefly, but with import, to a quarterly meeting Holmes attended shortly before his premature death:

> On Sabbath he attended a Quarterly Meeting with the African brethren, at the site of the town of Chatham, [Upper Canada] where he preached from Matthew v. 16 (sic), administered the Lord's Supper, and walked home in the evening about five miles, to all appearances enjoying an unusual degree of health.[34]

Carroll gave another account of the Lord's Supper (1828) and its spiritual impact in a celebration in an indigenous community:

> 'The elder [William Case] proceeded to administer the holy communion of the Lord's Supper, of which 85 0f the natives partook. The power of the Lord rested upon the assembly, and at the close of this service an overwhelming shower of Divine grace descended upon us, and there was a mighty shout in the house. Our Presiding Elder was full of joy and joined the Indians in their praises to God.[35]

---

[33] Carroll. Case, 1: 234.
[34] Carroll. Case, 1:266.
[35] Carroll. Case, 3: 174.

We also find this enthusiastic report of a camp meeting Communion at Belleville, Upper Canada, in 1834:

> During my religious experience I have never witnessed quite such a meeting, and I believe the most experienced Christians on the ground would agree in making the same remark. I do not now refer to the numbers converted or awakened, but to the peculiar baptism of the Holy Spirit which so signally characterized this meeting. [After describing the camp meeting generally, the narrative continues:] The Lord however had, as it proved, reserved the best wine to the last day of the feast. On Monday evening, according to arrangements made, the holy sacrament of the Lord's Supper was to be administered after a sermon by the Presiding Elder. But the elder preached not; for during the introductory prayer, Heaven came down to earth. An uncommon, an indescribable, and an overwhelming shower of Divine grace. It was indeed a 'new and more abundant effusion of the Holy Spirit.' The ministers of the sanctuary and the membership were alike watered; both in the stand and in the congregation there were those who like John when overwhelmed with the presence and glory of Jesus, 'fell as dead.' For the space of an hour all was rejoicing and praise, in a sense quite beyond description. I dare say we made a noise; a noise in miniature similar to the sounds with which Heaven will be filled when the bride and the church dwells at home in the house above, when the unnumbered multitude will praise with a 'loud voice,' (Rev. 7th and 19th chapters.) It was evident too that the Spirit's operations were not confined to the people of God; for when the holy sacrament had been administered to many happy saints of God, and a goodly number of awakened sinners, an invitation was given to the penitents to come to the altar, when nearly fifty persons presented themselves as burdened and heavy laden; for whom prayer was made; nor was it made in vain.[36] (Carroll. Case, 3: 464-465.)

This exuberant report holds a great deal of what we might call spiritual information. Here we have the kinds of transformation at the center of Wesley's theology and Methodism's mission, flowing from the power of the Spirit as people encounter the living God. Here partakers anticipate heaven above in their "heaven

---

[36] Carroll. Case, 3: 464-465.

below."[37] Here every barrier, burden, distraction, and division is swept away by the "overwhelming shower of Divine grace." Here every earthly concern and human priority is put in proper perspective as "Heaven came down to earth." Here the ingredients of Christ's presence come together: memory, promise, and the power of the Spirit.

---

[37] Lester Ruth, *Heaven Below*.

Chapter 5

"Until he Comes" (II Corinthians 11:26, ESV)

As powerful as were the Lord's Suppers in the pioneer days of North American Methodism, the Eucharist was intended for many generations, not just for a few decades. By 1859, at least in some areas, the place and manner of Holy Communion had begun to weaken among Methodists. That was the year Samuel Luckey [1791-1869] published *The Lord's Supper*, a wake-up call to the Methodist Episcopal clergy and people to take serious notice and action regarding a Sacrament in stages of decline.

No doubt some found his warning surprising or overdone, but others, like Bishop Edmund Janes [1807-1876], who wrote the book's introduction, recognized the problem and appreciated the warning. The bishop wrote that "the author aims to guide, and encourage, and aid the Christian in a proper and profitable observance of the holy sacrament, a duty by many members of the Church but imperfectly understood, by some wholly neglected, and by others observed with but little profit." Janes is convinced that if the author accomplishes his purpose, his book "must advance the faith, and spirituality, and steadfastness of the Church." Sadly, it appears that while it is "the Scriptural and sacred duty of all believers to observe this sacrament," somehow its observance was failing to produce its intended transformation. If the sacrament is "imperfectly understood" by many participants, "wholly neglected" by some, and experienced "with little profit" by others, the church has a problem!

Luckey sees very clearly why the problem is serious and why a remedy is needed. First, Holy Communion is not a burden or an insignificant option. It is God's good gift, a means of grace designed "to strengthen the faith" of those who receive it and "promote their growth in grace." Luckey says that this Supper "embraces all the fundamental doctrines of the Gospel" and presents them to us in a powerful way. Most profoundly,

> It is God's own institution, in which he has promised to meet with his people, to renew his covenant of mercy and grace with them, and to edify and strengthen them in the divine life. As a means of grace eminently adapted to advance believers in piety and holiness, the primitive disciples of Christ devoutly observed it as a part, and the principal part of their service every time they met for worship.[1]

Here Luckey echoes John Wesley' insistent plea that the Eucharist is both blessing and command - reasons enough to warrant thankful obedience. Luckey's reference to the place of Communion in the worship of the early Church – "the primitive disciples of Christ" – also echoes Wesley.

How and why did parts of the Methodist family drift so far from Wesley's British and Irish converts who swamped parish churches in order to receive the Lord's Supper? What happened to those who found thundering oceans of transforming power in the Communion celebrations at the end of quarterly and camp meetings? First it is important not to over-generalize, but also important to take it seriously as pointing to a widespread malaise with a lasting impact on many churches.

A comprehensive look at the situation of Methodism in the late 1850s shows that a decline in Eucharistic practice was only one of many parallel concerns.[2] Changes in the Church often mirrored

---

[1] Samuel Luckey. The Lord's Supper. New York, NY; Phillips & Hunt; Cincinnati, OH: 1859, iv; 3-4.

[2] Howard A. Snyder. *Populist Saints: B.T. and Ellen Roberts and the First Free Methodists.* Grand Rapids, MI: Eerdmans, 2006; Kevin Watson. *Old or New School Methodism (etc.)* Oxford, UK: Oxford University Press, 2019.

changes in society. It would be interesting and instructive to see how major reform movements, such as The National Camp Meeting Association for the Promotion of Holiness [1867ff.], dealt with this matter. Even more to the point is for us to explore possibilities for renewal of our own Eucharistic understanding and practice in light of what we have seen in North America's early Methodist movement.

The Lord's Supper was so important in the life of the church and its preachers that they marked as memorable milestones both the first time a minister celebrated the sacrament and the first time it was celebrated in a particular place. Thus we read Billy Hibbard's [1771-1844] account of his "consideration that I was not holy enough to administer the sacraments." His wrestling ended when,

> This plea was taken from me, so that I dare not make it any more before God, on this wise: one night (after a very happy day in communion with God) I dreamed that I came out of a woods, into an open field of most delightful green pasture, where I saw all the members of my class were assembled around a table. My heart leaped for joy to see them. I asked them why they were there. They said, "brother, we have been waiting for you to come and administer the sacrament to us; we have the elements of bread and wine here all prepared; and we want you to make the prayer of consecration, and administer it to us; for the Lord has made us all happy." I thought I saw their spirits shining with love to God; and I was also very happy, so that I could not resist with any propriety. I therefore said, let us pray,-we all kneeled down around the table, and I lifted up my hands and eyes to heaven, and began to pray for the presence of God to be with us; and as I looked up, I saw heaven open, and Jesus at the right hand of God, and the heavenly host surrounding the throne, adoring the Father and Son in the most sublime strains.- at this sight my soul caught the heavenly fire, and I began to clap my hands, and cried out, Glory! glory! glory! glory! ... I thought, why has the Lord given me this blessed dream. The impression immediately came;- to show you that you ought not to object to preach, or say that you are not fit to administer the sacraments; for whom God calls he qualifies:

only trust in him, and your way will be plain.[3]

Francis Asbury referred to the synergy of the Lord's Supper in this comment from 1780: I attended the communion – communicants increase daily, for people get awakened by us; when this is the case, they go to the Lord's supper.[4]

James Finley contrasted the joy of his first experience with receiving Communion with his handling of a milestone, struggle and victory experience leading worship, including Communion. Both reveal significant attitudes and approaches to the Eucharistic experience.

> In the afternoon the sacrament of the Lord's supper was administered; and as I never had partaken of this holy communion before, it was a time of great self-examination, and deliberate, solemn consecration to God on my part. I was much blessed in partaking of the emblems of the broken body and shed blood of my redeemer.
>
> ...
>
> It was with considerable difficulty that I consented to attempt the task [of temporarily supplying the place of his absent presiding elder], yet with great depression of mind I entered upon the work.... I was made to realize my trust in God and the necessity of greater spiritual power. I prayed with earnestness for the baptism of the Holy Spirit, and in reconsecrating my heart to God I felt the power divine. O the ineffable riches and extent of divine love! May my soul ever bask in its infinite ocean! At the first quarterly meeting, during the holy communion, the Spirit was poured out in rich effusion.[5]

George Playter relayed this account of circuit preacher Darius Dunham [1762-1825] and the first Methodist Communion in Upper Canada, in 1792:

---

[3] Billy Hibbard. Memoirs of the Life and Travels of B. Hibbard. New-York, NY: Printed and Published for the Author, 1825, 118.

[4] Francis Asbury. *Journal*, I:358.

[5] W.P. Strickland, ed. Autobiography of Rev. James B. Finley (etc.). Cincinnati, OH: Cranston & Curts; New York, NY: Hunt & Eaton, 1853, 186; 277.

No quarterly meetings had yet been held, no sacraments administered, nor matrimony solemnized. But the Methodists were now to enjoy all the privileges of a regular church. ...it was agreed to have a quarterly meeting, as the Methodists had in the United States. ... Darius Dunham, preacher in charge of the circuit, acted in place of the presiding elder. On the Sunday, we may imagine the new Methodists of the six townships, ... devoutly going in to the first love-feast in the province, beholding the two preachers at the table. After the love-feast, the Methodists see the broken bread and the cup, for the first time, in the hands of a Methodist preacher, - who earnestly invites them to draw near and partake of the holy sacrament to their comfort. A new and solemn ordinance for them.[6]

Two accounts of the first Eucharist under the auspices of Methodists in Ohio seem to conflict with one another. One credits John Kobler [1768-1843] as the earliest. The account favoring Kobler indicates that he,

...on the second of August, 1798, preached the first sermon in the territory by a regularly constituted Methodist missionary. He administered the sacrament of the Lord's supper at a regularly appointed quarterly meeting at Mrs. McCormick's, held on the twenty-fourth and twenty-fifth days of December, 1798. This was the first time the Methodists had partaken of the sacrament in the territory.[7]

James Finley [1783-1857], pioneer and biographer of Ohio Methodism reminisced about "the time when he spread the first table for the sacrament of the Lord's supper that was spread northwest of the Ohio. When the communicants were called to approach the table, the number did not exceed twenty-five or thirty; this is the sum total of all that were in the country." Whichever account is more reliable, they both make the same point in highlighting the importance of "firsts" and the Lord's Supper.[8]

---

[6] George F. Playter. The History of Methodism in Canada (etc.).Toronto, ON: Anson Green, for the Author, 1862, 35.

[7] John M'lean, ed. Sketch of Rev. Philip Gatch. Cincinnati, OH: Swormstedt & Poe, 1854, 138.

[8] W.P. Strickland, ed. *Sketches of Western Methodism (etc.)*. Cincinnati, OH: Methodist Book Concern, for the Author, 1856, 171.

One measure of the impact of a camp meeting, including its closing Communion, was how hard it was to leave. Joseph Long [1800 -1869] recorded a departure that he found especially difficult:

> We celebrated the Lord's Supper, and closed our meeting under the mighty influences of divine grace. Now came the time of parting. I must say adieu to Bro. Klinefelter.... This parting touched me painfully, for I was now left alone on this field of labor and had a great many crosses and trials to bear. I began to think that I would rather depart and be with Christ than to remain longer in this world. But I tried to comfort my heart in God by considering how he had helped me hitherto.[9]

Bishop Long's was a very personal reflection. A more complete and universal account comes from Nathan Bangs,[1778-1862], who became the premier historian of early American Methodism. Bangs spent several of his early years in ministry in Canada, and so was well prepared to record chapters from the history of Canadian Methodism, especially during its formative period. Much of what he wrote about Canada's first camp meeting I include here to provide the context for the eventual departure of preachers and people from the camp ground, and to give something of the flavor of this event and many that followed.

> [The] first "camp-meeting" in Canada [1805] was held in Adolphustown, where the first Methodist class of the province was organized, in 1790, by its first Methodist preacher, William Losee, and its first Methodist chapel erected in 1792. Camp-meetings had been extensively held in the Western United States for about five years.
>
> ... The first camp meeting in Canada appeared to Dr. Bangs a salient fact in the history of Canadian Methodism. He therefore made particular notes respecting it. ... It was attended by extraordinary displays of the favor and power of God.
>
> Its announcement beforehand excited great interest far and near.

---

[9] R. Yeakel. Bishop Joseph Long, the Peerless Preacher of the Evangelical Association. Cleveland, OH: Thomas & Mattill, 1897, 27.

Whole families prepared for a pilgrimage to the ground. Processions of wagons and of foot passengers wended along the highways. With two of his fellow-evangelists, our itinerant had to take his course from a remote appointment through a range of forest thirty miles in extent. They hastened forward, conversing on religious themes, praying or singing, and eager with expectation of the moral battle scene about to open. [Once the meeting was fully underway,] ... the Spirit of the Lord seemed to move among the people. After an interruption of an hour and a half a prayer-meeting was held, and toward its close the power of God descended on the assembly, and songs of victory and praise resounded through the forest. The battle thus opened, the exercises continued with preaching, exhorting, and singing until midnight, when the people retired to their booths. The night was clear and serene, and the scene being new to us, a peculiar solemnity rested upon all minds. The lights glowing among the trees and above the tents, and the voice of prayer and praise, mingling and ascending into the star-lit night, altogether inspired the heart with emotions better felt than described. During this day six persons passed from death to life [John 5:24].

[by 10:00 the next morning,] the congregation had increased to perhaps twenty-five hundred, and the people of God were seated on logs near the stand, while a crowd were standing in a semicircle around them. During the sermon I felt an unusual sense of the divine presence, and thought I could see a cloud of divine glory resting upon the congregation. [In the midst of his sermon the preacher noticed movement in the congregation and stopped in his tracks. Bangs, who had been up in the stand, left his place to join the congregation.] The rest of the preachers all spontaneously followed me, and we went among the people, exhorting the impenitent and comforting the distressed; for while Christians were filled with "joy unspeakable and full of glory," many a sinner was weeping and praying in the surrounding crowd. These we collected together in little groups, and exhorted God's people to join in prayer for them, and not to leave them until he should save their souls. O what a scene of tears and prayer was this!

[Bangs goes into detail on how this praying arranged itself and its effect on those being prayed for.] The wicked looked on in silent amazement while they beheld some of their companions struck

> down by the mighty power of God, and heard his people pray for them. The mingled voices of prayer and praise were heard afar off and produced a solemn awe apparently upon all minds. [After continuing his comments on the impact of the day's worship, he indicates that there was more religious excitement to follow.] The meeting continued all night, and few, I think, slept that night. During this time some forty persons were converted or sanctified.
>
> [A beautiful Sunday morning followed, which corresponded perfectly with the joyful mood of the camp.] After breakfast ... we held a love-feast. The interest and excitement were so great, and the crowd so large that while some assembled around the stand, a preacher mounted a wagon at a distance and addressed a separate congregation. The impression of the Word was universal, the power of the Spirit was manifest throughout the whole encampment, and almost every tent was a scene of prayer. At noon the Lord's supper was administered to multitudes, while other multitudes looked on in astonishment and tears.

Unfortunately, and strangely, given Bangs' detail about so much of the event, he tells us no more about the sacrament. Caution is advised when arguing from silence, yet it seems safe to say that, in the absence of information to the contrary, the Lord's Supper shared the same tone as the rest of the gathering. People were moved in the presence and power of God and Communion contributed to the overall success of the meeting.

At any rate, the main purpose in relaying this story is to witness the departure of particpants when it was over, in order to realize how much the experience meant to preachers and people who were there.

> The time was at hand at last for the conclusion of the meeting. The last night was the most awfully impressive and yet delightful scene my eyes ever beheld. There was not a cloud on the sky. The stars studded the firmament, and the glory of God filled the camp. All the neighboring forest seemed vocal with the echoes of hymns. Turn our attention whichever way we could, we heard the voice of prayer or praise. As it was the last night, every moment seemed precious; parents were praying for their children or children for their parents, brothers and sisters for one another,

neighbors for neighbors, all anxious that before they left the consecrated ground they should be "sealed" as "heirs of salvation." I will not attempt to describe the parting scene, for it was indescribable. The preachers, about to disperse to their distant and hard fields of labor, hung about each other's necks weeping and yet rejoicing. Christians from remote settlements, who had here formed holy friendships which they suspected would survive in heaven, parted probably to meet no more on earth, but in joyful hope of reunion above. They wept, prayed, sang, shouted aloud, and had at last to break away from one another as by force. As the hosts marched off in different directions the songs of victory rolled along the highways. Great was the good that followed. A general revival of religion spread around the circuits, especially that of the Bay of Quinte, on which this meeting was held. I returned to Augusta circuit and renewed my labors, somewhat worn but full of the Holy Ghost.[10]

We can be grateful to the circuit riders who somehow managed to preserve in writing some of their memorable experiences, especially those dealing with transformative encounters with God in worship. Here is one such description from a little known writer, H.C. Wooster [1771-1798], from a quarterly meeting in Upper Canada:

> During the administration of the Lord's supper the Holy ghost seemed to overshadow them; and as the people came up to the commemorate the death of their dear Saviour, a risen Jesus met them in great power, so that three or four at once were deprived of their bodily strength by their great sense of the goodness of him who died for sinners. These had to be carried away to make room for others; and so it continued with some in almost every company that successively approached the table of the Lord. Did not these humble disciples, amid the forests of Upper Canada, enjoy the presence of that same almighty Saviour whose glory caused St. John, in the rocky isle of Patmos, to fall at his feet as dead, and who enabled him, amid all his privations, to sing, "Unto him that loved us, and washed us from our sins in his own blood, and that made us kings and priests unto God and his Father, to him be

---

[10] Abel Stevens. Life and Times of Nathan Bangs, D.D. New York, NY: Carlton & Porter, 1863, 151-155.

glory and dominion forever?[11]

Evangelical Association historian W.W. Orwig [1810-89] preserved this story of a camp meeting Communion in Pennsylvania. Quoting Presiding Elder H. Buck:

> We had three camp meetings in June, all of which were crowed with awakenings and conversions of sinners, and glorious revivals among the people of God. At the last of these meetings in Brush Valley, Indiana County, we had on the last day, during the celebration of the Lord's supper, and after that at an experience meeting, glorious times; it seemed as if heaven had opened over us, and the grace of God were descending upon us in showers so abundantly that the praise of God flowed from many lips, and some actually fell down, overcome by the love of God. (W.W. Orwig. History of the Evangelical Association. Cleveland, OH: Charles Hammer,1858, I:308.)

A much shorter account showing some similarity to Orwig's comes to us from John Seybert [1791-1860]. "Breakthrough was Seybert's term to describe our immersion into the depths /of grace, and he prized deep rather than superficial conversion. Here we have his summary of the core of an 1835 camp meeting: "At a camp meeting near Orwigsburg, Pennsylvania, ... in the preparation service of the Lord's supper, some sank as though dead, into the great sea of God's love.[12]

Christian Newcomer recorded a time when...

> Heaven opened above, and the aweful [awesome] presence of God was there and filled the house with glory. The devout worshipers appeared to be carried away involuntarily with the swelling emotions of the moment, and as if compelled by an invisible power, they all began to pray aloud; and my voice was soon lost in the mingled cries of the multitude.

This exercise continued about one hour without any intermis-

---

[11] Memoir of Rev. H.C. Wooster, in Elbert Osborne . Passages in the Life and Ministry of Elbert Osborne. Published by the Author, 1850, 232; Revelation 1:6.

[12] John Steven O'Malley. *John Seybert and the Evangelical Heritage*. Lexington, KY: Emeth, 2008, 105.

sion. As it commenced without any notice, so there would be no sign by which I could decide when the excitement would cease. It was altogether undesigned [sic] and unexpected; and therefore not "got up," as it is believed some excitements are – there was nothing mechanical in its cause. A supernatural impulse fell upon the people; we all felt it, and knew that it was the work of the Lord. So I did not lift a hand to steady thee ark, or try to stop the people from praying. Even opposers to noisy exercises said nothing against that wonderful work of God. Indeed, the occurrence was new and surprising to me. ... At length, however, the solemn sound in the concert of prayer began to sink into a dying cadence, and then suddenly came to a close. Immediately afterward I entered the desk, and preached under the influence of divine power.[13]

The dramatic scenes that many reported in early Methodist Communions stand in marked contrast to the Communions many experience today. Descriptions of changed lives through powerful outpourings of the Spirit, expressed in strong emotions and sometimes wild behavior must appear exotic and perhaps off-putting from such a great distance in time. Or is the problem that we expect too little from the Lord's Supper today, so that too many of our present day Communions are living down to our expectations – certainly not always, but too often? What should we hope for when we gather at the Lord's table? What connects our experiences at the altar with those we have seen from the days of the Wesleys or the early North American Methodists?

Surely we are in no position to expect, in the sense of demand, anything from God in this regard. But just as surely, we can expect, meaning look forward to, everything God has promised to deliver through this means of grace. Among them are these:

> **+ God will be there to meet us** at his table and in the fellowship around the table. "I am the bread of life. ... Whoever eats this bread will live forever. This bread is my flesh, which I will give for the life of the world. ... whoever eats my flesh and drinks my blood has eternal life. (John 6: 48, 51-54, NIV) there are two gifts here – **Christ's presence and eternal life** – both offered in the

---

[13] Newcomer. Journal, 241- 242.

present.

+ **God will forgive** us when we come to him in penitence. "This is my blood of the covenant, which is poured out for many for the forgiveness of sins." (Matthew 26:28, NIV) forgiveness is a priceless blessing, lifting burdens in the present and removing chains from our future.

+ **God stands ready to heal and reconcile** broken and damaged relationships. "His purpose was to create in himself one new humanity out of the two, thus making peace." (I Ephesians 2:15, NIV) The original context was division between Jews and gentiles, but the message is applicable in other cases.

+ **God can strengthen** us for our journey. "God is our refuge and strength;" "Wait on the Lord; Be of good courage, And he shall strengthen your heart; Wait, I say, on the Lord!"[14]

+ God will be there with **wisdom and power to reorient and redirect** our lives. Jesus sent the Holy Spirit to teach and guide us, orienting our lives in him who is "the way and the truth and the life." (John 14: 16-18; 14:6, NIV) He can focus our thoughts and dispel our distractions.

+ God's **sanctifying grace** will be available to transform our lives. God's ultimate purpose for us is an eternal, infinite, hope-filled future built upon grace. As a major means of grace, the Eucharist is a gift of hope. Change is a natural part of every encounter with God, which is especially focused at the Lord's table.

Neither are we in any position to create or control encounters with God in Holy Communion. Yet we can, prompted by grace, cultivate attitudes and approaches of availability and responsiveness to God. Some crucial spiritual elements for experiencing and benefiting from God's presence at the Lord's table are:

+**Perceptivity** – recognition of signs of his presence; resisting intrusive distractions; paying attention. Just as heaven reflects God's attributes of eternity and infinity, those same attributes

---

[14] Psalm 46:1, NIV; Psalm 27:14, NKJV).

characterize the essence of the Communion experience for those who seek him. The sacrament is one way to "set [our] minds on things above, not on earthly things."[15]

+Receptivity – openness and eagerness to welcome him and to accept, enjoy, and appreciate his blessings, one of which is wisdom, for "in [Christ] are hidden all the treasures of wisdom and knowledge." (Colossians 2:3, NIV)

+Engagement of the whole person, including the emotions. In early Methodist Communions, people were often shaken beyond superficial participation, so that God could reach, move, and transform them at the deepest level of their being. "Love the Lord your God with all your heart and with all your soul and with all your mind and with all your strength." (Mark 12:30, NIV)

+Discernment – understanding the meaning of the encounter as a step in the spiritual journey; sensing the glory of God. "For anyone who eats and drinks without discerning the body eats and drinks judgment on himself," (I Corinthians 11:29, ESV, a difficult verse on the importance of perceiving the meaning and purpose of the sacred meal, especially the sacrifice it represents and the real presence of Christ it conveys. Paul found the Corinthians misusing the Lord's Supper as an ordinary meal eaten in such a way as to accentuate class distinctions among fellow partakers.)

+Koinonia – fellowship with other participants. "intense unity and love" (Ruth, Heaven Below, 159.) God's interaction with each of us is highly personal, though we travel the road to glory together. Both dimensions must be developed in balance.

+Synergy – divine initiative and personal response in continuous interaction. In John 13:14-15 Jesus models servant leadership by washing his disciples' feet, a practice some churches continue as part of Holy (Maundy) Thursday Communion services.

The liturgies we use should assist us in all these things. To accomplish this the liturgies should not be overly brief, superficial, or casual, signifying a lack of importance or depth. Nor should

---

[15] Adam Clarke. Christian Theology. New-York: G. Lane & P.P. Sandford, 1842, 64; 66; 376-380; Colossians 3:2, NIV.

they be overly long or ponderous, to the point where they invite boredom or exhaustion. Instead, they need to embody the power and grace, joy and serious purpose intrinsic to the sacrament. In churches that allow or encourage freedom and creativity, the liturgical traditions offer rich resources for constructing rich and meaningful worship.

I close with my favorite story of a true wilderness Communion, an experience recounted by Henry C. Benson [1815-97] and the inspiration for this book and its title:

> [On their travels across the American South,] carried by the tide of emigration as it continued to roll westward, headed for Indian territory, a mixed band of whites and Choctaws stopped in the forest of the Ozark mountains to hold a camp meeting [one that would feature an unusual communion.] We had a love-feast , and then preaching in the evening, at the close of which it was thought proper to administer the sacrament of the Lord's supper to the few disciples who were there convened. "But could we have the elements in that remote and wilderness locality?" Yes; a brother had already gone to the woods and procured a few clusters of wild grapes, which were found upon a forest tree. They were of an excellent quality, almost equal in flavor to the Catawba or Isabella. These were pressed to furnish the wine, giving a pure and genuine article…. The bread was procured and the wine was served to the communicants, at the altar, in a teacup, as there were no glass tumblers on the ground, and probably none in that section of the country. About twenty of the professed disciples of the Lord kneeled upon the ground, at the rude bench, to commemorate the dying sorrows of our crucified but risen Savior. It was an occasion full of interest and solemnity, and never had the Eucharistic feast appeared to us more solemn, impressive, and spiritual than there and then, with the starry canopy above and the curtain of darkness drawn around us.[16]

There was a special poignancy about a wilderness Communion like the one Benson and his fellow travelers shared that night. No matter how isolated the place, and no matter how large or small the number of participants, the experience could be transformed

---

[16] Henry C. Benson. Life Among the Choctaw Indians (etc,). Cincinnati, OH: Swormstedt & Poe, 1860,143-144.

in profound and powerful ways by the presence of the Lord. Hooper Crews [b. 1807] was a pioneer in Illinois, when obliged to go on foot forty-five miles without ... getting any refreshments, and at the end of such a route, on one occasion, to administer the sacrament to a man and his wife who dwelt alone in the wilderness, and with whom in this blessed rite he enjoyed a higher satisfaction than he would in being possessor of the town of Rockford, in which he now lived....[17]

George Brown [1792-1871] provided a helpful perspective in this comment on Communion at quarterly conference on a remote, mountainous circuit:

> Next followed the holy communion, attended by a rich flow of heavenly feeling. It was a time of refreshing from the presence of the Lord. City Christians, who have this privilege once a month, can hardly form an idea of a communion season among mountain Christians, who rarely have it oftener than twice a year.
>
> When the congregation was dismissed, they all sat down again, and seemed loth to leave the place. (George Brown. Recollections of Itinerant Life (etc.).Cincinnati, OH: R.W. Carroll, 1866, 334.)

---

[17] John I. Smith. *Indiana Methodism (etc.)*, Valparaiso, IN, n.p., 1892, n.p.

Appendix

Fencing the Lord's Table

What follows is a miscellany of references to the Eucharist in early North American Methodism, items that shed further light on this important part of its life and worship.

We have already seen the concern of Bishops Coke and Asbury to guard the Lord's Supper from misuse through offering it carelessly. One way of organizing this concern was to limit those qualified to administer the sacrament. This polity statement from Bishop Robert Paine's biography of Bishop William McKendree lays out rules concerning the roles of various categories of those in ministries in episcopal Methodism.

> We do not suffer one officer in the Church of God to assume or invade the rights of another; a licensed exhorter to be always attempting to preach; a traveling or local preacher must not baptize without ordination; a deacon, traveling or local, to administer the Lord's supper, but under the order of an elder. On no account will we suffer the elders to ordain alone, but to come forward when called upon by the bishop ... to assist in the ordination of elders. We do not suffer our presiding elders to invade any singular right of episcopacy. (Robert Paine. Life and Times of William McKendree (etc.). Nashville, TN; Dallas, TX; Richmond, VA: Publishing House Methodist Episcopal Church South, 1922, 442.)

George Coles [1792-1858] describes the normal way unordained preachers dealt with restrictions on their ability to officiate at sacraments, while still making them available to their people: "As the young preacher was not ordained, he frequently called on me to administer the ordinances of baptism and the Lord's supper, and more than overfetched me in his wagon to perform the office of matrimony."[1]

James Finley served for several years as Chaplain for the Ohio State Prison in Columbus.. He took very seriously the spiritual well-being of the inmates and had great hopes for their thorough rehabilitation. To that end, as we saw earlier, he wanted to provide a sacramental ministry to them, but was prevented from doing so by prison policy and public attitudes. This was a case of a Methodiist preacher trying to remove unnecessary and counterproductive fencing around what should have been a means of transforming grace, built on Finleys compassionate, evangelistic vision. He wanted a merciful society toopen the door to the captive, that he may enjoy the benefits of the Gospel of peace -- that his chains may fall off, and that he may be set free by the power of the Holy Spirit. Let him have all the means of grace and Gospel ordinances.[2] There were times when early Methodist preachers believed it to be their responsibility to guard the integrity of the Lord's table by prohibiting those holding heretical doctrines from recieving Communion as part of their worship. Charles Giles [1783-1867] felt this kind of duty when confronted by an Arian seeking to partake during a quarterly meeting:

> The love feast as usual was attended with joy, and some spiritual animation; at the close of which the sacrament was administered. During that exercise, a certain lady came forward, expressing a desire to unite with us in the holy communion, stating at the same time that she was not a member of the Methodist society, and that her opinions respecting the divinity of Jesus Christ did not agree with the opinions of many on that subject. It evidently

---

[1] George Coles. *Incidents of My Later Years (etc.)*. New York, NY: Carlton & Phillips, 1853, 271.)

[2] B.F. Tefft, ed. *Memorials of Prison Life, by Rev. James B. Finley*. Cincinnati, OH: Swormstedt & Poe, 1855, 301-302.

appeared from her own statements that she was an Arian in her doctrinal views. Not feeling authorized to give my approval to such heretical doctrines by an act of cordial fellowship, I did not admit her to the communion table – the question was soon settled, and the service went on.

The Eucharistic ceremony being ended, we all knelt down to offer up the closing prayer. As I began my address to the throne of Heaven, the before-mentioned Arian woman came into remembrance and I prayed for her, personally, that she might be delivered from error, and be brought into the truth; that she might behold the glorious character of her Redeemer, who is "the true God, the mighty God – the Lord from heaven – the Creator of all things." Instantly, as I was speaking, a supernatural impulse was felt throughout the assembly,

In this case, the preacher was convinced of the correctness of his decision to maintain a doctrinal fence. The request from the Arian woman was forthright and honest, which eliminated some potential confusion. The incident is hard to transplant to our present situation, where most fencing has been rejected. Yet we can perhaps envision a private conversation in which the pastor could explain the difficulty with the person's request and help clear the way for her to see the truth and importance of orthodoxy. As much as the minister might want to be hospitable, he could not justify Arian Communion on theological or pastoral grounds, but he could offer genuine hospitality evangelistically.

James Finley tells a contrasting story involving Bishop William McKendree [1757-1835], in which the bishop's pastoral approach takes a very different direction which changes Finley's mind on the subject. But the issue is different, pointing to the necessity for celebrants to use discernment and flexibility in pastoral situations where the ultimate purpose is connecting people with the grace of God.(see the Finley narrative above in Chapter 4.}

There are references to Holy Communion that are of a personal nature. Among them are a conversion dream of Benjamin Abbott [1732-1796] and a deathbed request from Henry Bascom's

[1796-1850] father. Both indicate the profound importance of this sacrament at transitional moments in life.³

The Abbott dream is especially moving for this dreamer:

> O! that there were a minister to give me the Lord's supper! Then by faith I saw the Lord

> Jesus come to me as with a cup in his hand, and he gave it to me, and I took it and drank thereof: it was like unto honey for sweetness. At that moment the Scriptures were wonderfully opened to my understanding. I was now enabled to interpret the dream or vision to my own satisfaction.

All the settings, manners, rules, and responses associated with the Lord's Supper emphasized its importance to the Church and its people. That importance arose primarily from the real presence of Christ producing real change in the hearts, lives, and relationships of those taking part in the sacrament. That spiritual dynamic was especially pronounced when "God spread a table in the wilderness." (Psalm 78:19, ESV) There, in numbers large and small, the feasting was unmatched by anything this side of heaven.

There is no reason such feasting has to be left in times and places of long ago. if we ground our hopeful expectation on the One who is forever the same, he will still meet us at the table he spreads for us, in a church or wilderness of our own.

---

[3] John Ffirth. *Experience and Gospel Labors of the Rev. Benjamin Abbott*. New-York: T. Mason & G. Lane, 1836, 14; Moses Montgomery Henkle. *Life of Henry Bidleman Bascom*. Louisville, KY: Morton & Griswold, 1854, 242.

www.ingramcontent.com/pod-product-compliance
Lightning Source LLC
Chambersburg PA
CBHW071513150426
43191CB00009B/1507